THE ONE BIG THING

Copyright © 2019 CelebrityPress® LLC

All rights reserved. No part of this book may be used or reproduced in any manner whatsoever without prior written consent of the author, except as provided by the United States of America copyright law.

Published by CelebrityPress®, Orlando, FL.

CelebrityPress® is a registered trademark.

Printed in the United States of America.

ISBN: 978-0-9980369-9-1
LCCN: 2019908493

This publication is designed to provide accurate and authoritative information with regard to the subject matter covered. It is sold with the understanding that the publisher is not engaged in rendering legal, accounting, or other professional advice. If legal advice or other expert assistance is required, the services of a competent professional should be sought. The opinions expressed by the authors in this book are not endorsed by CelebrityPress® and are the sole responsibility of the author rendering the opinion.

Most CelebrityPress® titles are available at special quantity discounts for bulk purchases for sales promotions, premiums, fundraising, and educational use. Special versions or book excerpts can also be created to fit specific needs.

For more information, please write:
CelebrityPress®
520 N. Orlando Ave, #2
Winter Park, FL 32789
or call 1.877.261.4930

Visit us online at: www.CelebrityPressPublishing.com

THE ONE BIG THING

CelebrityPress®
Winter Park, Florida

CONTENTS

CHAPTER 1
CLARIFY YOUR VALUES
By Brian Tracy 11

CHAPTER 2
**SALES SECRETS OF THE SHY
AND INTROVERTED**
A ROADMAP FOR THOSE OF US WHO CAN'T STAND SELLING
By Jason Minion 23

CHAPTER 3
FROM A YELLOW DUCK TO A WHITE SWAN
By Mina Vo 35

CHAPTER 4
**FOUR CRITICAL MARKETING MISTAKES
THAT ARE DESTROYING YOUR PROFITS**
By Greg Rollett 45

CHAPTER 5
THE STATE OF YOUR SEO: TAKE A MINUTE AND TAKE STOCK
By Lindsay Dicks 55

CHAPTER 6
CHECK YOUR TICKET TO FINANCIAL FREEDOM
By Debbie Neumayer 63

CHAPTER 7
FINDING YOUR UNIQUE LEADERSHIP VOICE, ONE DECISION AT A TIME
By Evelyn Campos Diaz 73

CHAPTER 8
DICTION AND TONE SET THE TONE FOR YOUR BUSINESS
By Jamie Ziska, Executive Business Coach 81

CHAPTER 9
TRANSFORMING YOUR BUSINESS INTO A BLOCKBUSTER
By Nick Nanton and JW Dicks 89

CHAPTER 10
DIVORCE OR DESTINY
TRANSFORM YOUR LIFE BY PRESSING THE RESET BUTTON
By George Lee, Esq. 101

CHAPTER 11
LOVE-LIFE'S ONLY VALUABLE EMOTION
By Seema Choudhri 111

CHAPTER 12
PAINFREE ... WOW!™ - THE SHORTCUT TO INSTANT PAIN ELIMINATION
By Dr. Thay Joe Tan 123

CHAPTER 1

CLARIFY YOUR VALUES

BY BRIAN TRACY

One universe made up of all that is: and one God in it all, and one principle of being, and one law, the reason shared by all thinking creatures, and one truth.
~ Marcus Aurelius

One of the most important characteristics of leaders, and top people in every area of life, is that they know *who they are, what they believe in and what they stand for.* Average people are usually confused about their goals, values and ideals, and as a result, they go back and forth and accomplish very little. Men and women who become leaders, on the other hand, with the same or even fewer abilities and opportunities, go on to accomplish great things in whatever they attempt.

Life is lived from the inside out. The very core of your personality is your values. Your values are what make you the person you are. Everything you do on the outside is dictated and determined by your values on the inside, whether clear or fuzzy. The greater clarity you have regarding your values on the inside, the more precise and effective your actions will be on the outside.

THE FIVE LEVELS OF PERSONALITY

You can imagine your personality by thinking of a target with concentric rings, from the inside to the outside. Your personality is also made up of five rings, starting from the center, your values, and radiating outward to the next circle, your beliefs.

Your *values* determine your *beliefs*, about yourself and the world around you. If you have positive values, such as love, compassion and generosity, you will believe that people in your world are deserving of these values, and you will treat them accordingly.

EXPECT THE BEST

Your beliefs in turn determine the third ring of your personality, your expectations. If you have positive values, you will believe yourself to be a good person. If you believe yourself to be a good person, you will expect good things to happen to you. If you expect good things to happen to you, you will be positive, cheerful and future oriented. You will look for the good in other people and situations.

The fourth level of your personality, determined by your expectations, is your *attitude*. Your attitude will be an outward manifestation or reflection of your values, beliefs and expectations. For example, if your value is that this is a good world to live in, and your belief is that you are going to be very successful in life, you will *expect* that everything that happens to you is helping you in some way. As a result, you will have a positive mental attitude toward other people and they will respond positively toward you. You will be a more cheerful and optimistic person. You will be someone that others want to work with and for, buy from, sell to and generally help to be more successful. This is why a positive mental attitude seems to go hand in hand with great success in every walk of life.

The fifth ring, or level of life, is your *actions*. Your actions on the outside will ultimately be a reflection of your innermost values, beliefs and expectations on the inside. This is why what you achieve in life and work will be determined more by what is going on inside of you than by any other factor.

AS WITHIN, SO WITHOUT

You can always tell how a person thinks, most of the time, by looking at the conditions of their outer lives. A positive, optimistic, goal and future oriented person - on the inside - will enjoy a happy, successful and prosperous life on the outside, most of the time.

Aristotle said that the ultimate aim or purpose of human life is to achieve your own happiness. You are the very happiest when what you are doing on the outside is *congruent* with your values on the inside. When you are living in complete alignment with what you consider to be good and right and true, you will automatically feel happy and positive about yourself and your world.

Your goals must be congruent with your values, and your values must be congruent with your goals. This is why clarifying your values is often the starting point to high achievement and peak performance. Values clarification requires that you think through what is really important to you in life. You then organize your entire life around these values.

Any attempt to live on the outside in a manner that contradicts the values you hold on the inside will cause you stress, negativity, unhappiness, pessimism and even anger and frustration. Your chief responsibility to yourself in the creation of a great life is therefore for you to develop absolute clarity about your values in everything you do.

KNOW WHAT YOU REALLY WANT

Stephen Covey once said, *"Be sure that, as you scramble up the ladder of success, it is leaning against the right building."* Peggy Lee once sang a famous line, *"Is that all there is?"* Many people work hard on the outside to achieve goals that they think they want, only to find, at the end of the day, that they get no joy or satisfaction from their accomplishments. This occurs when the outer accomplishment is not in harmony with your inner values. Don't let this happen to you.

Socrates said, *"The unexamined life is not worth living."* This applies to your values as much as to any other area of your life. Values clarification is something you do on a "go-forward" basis. You continually stop the clock, like a time out in a football game, and ask, "What are my values in this area?"

In the Bible it says, *"What does it benefit a man if he achieves the whole world but loses his own soul?"* The happiest people in the world today are those who are living in harmony with their innermost convictions and values. The unhappiest people are those who are attempting to live incongruent with what they truly value and believe.

TRUST YOUR INTUITION

Self-trust is the foundation of greatness. Self-trust comes from listening to your intuition, to your "still, small voice" within. Men and women begin to become great when they begin to listen to their inner voices, and absolutely trust that they are being guided by a higher power, each step of the way.

Living in alignment with your true values is the royal road to self-confidence, self-respect and personal pride. In fact, almost every human problem can be resolved by returning to values. Whenever you experience stress of any kind, look into yourself and ask, *"In what way am I compromising my innermost values in this situation?"*

WATCH YOUR BEHAVIOR

How can you tell what your values really are? The answer is simple. You always demonstrate your true values in your *actions*, and especially your actions *under pressure*. Whenever you are forced to choose between one behavior and another, you will always act consistent with what is most important and valuable to you at that moment.

Values, in fact, are organized in a hierarchy. You have a series of values, some of them very intense and important, and some of them weaker and less important. One of the most important exercises you can engage in, to determine *who* you really are, and *what* you really want, is to organize your values by priority. Once you are clear about the relative importance of your values, you can then organize your outer life so that it is in alignment with them.

EXAMINE YOUR PAST BEHAVIOR

There are some insightful ways to help you to determine your true values. First of all, you can look at your past. How have you behaved under pressure in the past? What choices did you make with your time or money when you were forced to choose? Your answers will give you an indication of your predominant values at that time.

Dale Carnegie once wrote, *"Tell me what gives a person his greatest feeling of importance, and I will tell you his entire philosophy of life."* What makes you feel important? What raises your self-esteem? What increases your sense of self-respect and personal pride? What have you accomplished in your past life that has given you the greatest sense of pride and satisfaction? These answers will give you good indications of your true values.

DETERMINE YOUR HEART'S DESIRE

The spiritual teacher, Emmet Fox, wrote about the importance of discovering your *"Heart's Desire."* What is your heart's desire? What is it that, deep down in your heart, more than anything else, you would like to be, have or do in life? As a friend of mine asks, *"What do you want to be famous for?"*

What words would you like people to use to describe you when you are not there? What would you like people to say about you when you have passed on? What would you like someone to say about you at your funeral? How do you want your family, friends and children to remember you? How would you want them to talk about you after you had left this earth? How would you like people to talk to them about you?

What kind of a reputation do you have today? What kind of a reputation would you like to have sometime in the future? What would you have to begin doing today in order to create the kind of reputation that you desire?

YOUR PAST IS NOT YOUR FUTURE

Many people have had difficult experiences growing up. They have fallen onto hard times and become associated with the wrong people. They have behaved in ways that were illegal or socially unacceptable. Sometimes they have even been convicted and sent to prison for their crimes. But at a certain point in life, they decided to change. They thought seriously about the kind of person that they wanted to be known as, and thought of, in the future. They decided to change their lives by changing the values that they lived by. By making these decisions and sticking to them, they changed their lives. And what others have done, you can do as well.

Remember, *"It doesn't matter where you're coming from; all that really matters is where you're going."*

CLARIFY YOUR VALUES

If you were an outstanding person, in every respect, how would you behave toward others? What sort of impression would you leave on others after you had met them and spoken with them? Imagine you could be a completely excellent person, how would you be different from today?

HOW MUCH YOU LIKE YOURSELF

In psychology, your level of **self-esteem** determines your level of happiness. Self-esteem is defined as: "How much you like yourself." Your self-esteem, in turn, is determined by your self-image. This is the way you see yourself and think about yourself in your day-to-day interactions with others. Your **self-image** is shaped by your **self-ideal**. Your self-ideal is made up of the virtues, values, goals, hopes, dreams and aspirations that you have for yourself sometime in the future.

Here is what psychologists have discovered: The more your behavior in the moment is consistent with what you feel your *ideal* behavior should be, the more you like and respect yourself, and the happier you are.

On the other hand, whenever you behave in a way that is *inconsistent* with your ideal of your very best behavior, you experience a negative self-image. You feel yourself to be performing below your best, below what you truly aspire to. As a result, your self-esteem and your level of happiness decrease.

PERFORM AT YOUR BEST

The moment that you begin walking, talking and behaving in ways that are consistent with your highest ideals, your self-image improves, your self-esteem increases and you feel happier about yourself and your world. For example, whenever you are complimented or praised by another person, or given a prize or an award for accomplishment, your self-esteem goes up, sometimes dramatically. You feel happy about yourself. You feel that your whole life is in harmony, and that you are living congruent with your highest ideals. You feel successful and valuable.

Your aim should be to deliberately and systematically create the circumstances that raise your self-esteem in everything you do. You should live your life as if you were already the outstanding person that you intend to be sometime in the future.

KNOW WHAT YOU BELIEVE

What are your values today with regard to your *work* and your *career*? Do you believe in the values of integrity, hard work, dependability, creativity, cooperation, initiative, ambition, and getting along well with people? People who live these values in their work are vastly more successful and more highly esteemed than people who do not.

What are your values with regard to your *family*? Do you believe in the importance of unconditional love, continuous encouragement and reinforcement, patience, forgiveness, generosity, warmth and attentiveness? People who practice these values consistently with the important people in their lives are much happier than people who do not.

What are your values with regard to *money* and *financial success?* Do you believe in the importance of honesty, industry, thrift, frugality, education, excellent performance, quality and persistence? People who practice these values are far more successful in their financial lives than those who do not, and far faster as well.

What about your *health*? Do you believe in the importance of self-discipline, self-mastery, and self-control, with regard to diet, exercise and rest? Do you set high standards for your levels of health and fitness and then work every day to live up to those standards? People who practice these values live longer, healthier lives than people who do not.

THINK ONLY ABOUT WHAT YOU WANT

Remember, you become what you think about – most of the time. Successful, happy people think about their values, and how they can live and practice those values in every part of their lives, every single day. The big payoff is that, the more you live your life consistent with your values, the happier, healthier, more positive and energetic you will be.

BE TRUE TO YOURSELF

Perhaps the most important value of all is that of integrity. A billionaire once said to me, *"Integrity is not so much a value in itself; it is rather the value that guarantees all the other values."*

Wow! This was a great insight for me. Once you have decided that you are going to live consistent with a value, your level of integrity determines whether or not you follow through on your commitment. The more you discipline yourself to live consistent with the very best you know, the greater is your level of personal integrity. And the higher your level of integrity, the happier and more powerful you will feel in everything you do.

Truly great men and women are always described as having high levels of integrity. They live their lives consistent with their highest values, even when no one is looking. Mediocre men and women on the other hand, are always cutting corners and compromising their integrity, especially
when no one is watching.

LIVE IN TRUTH WITH YOURSELF AND OTHERS

Decide today to be a man or woman of *honor*. Resolve to tell the truth, and to live in truth with yourself and others. Crystallize your values in each area of your life. Write them down. Think of how you would behave if you were living consistent with those values, and then, refuse to compromise them for any reason.

Once you accept complete responsibility for your life, and for everything that happens to you, and then create an ideal picture of your perfect future and clarify your values, you are now ready to begin setting clear, specific goals in every area of your life. You are now on the launching ramp and ready to take off toward the stars.

Clarify Your Values:
1. Make a list of your 3-5 most important values in life today. What do you really believe in, and stand for?
2. What qualities and values are you best known for today among the people who know you?
3. What do you consider to be the most important values guiding your relationships with others in your life?
4. What are your values regarding money and financial success? Are you practicing these values daily?
5. Describe your picture of an ideal person, the person you would most want to be, if you had no limitations?
6. Write your own obituary, to be read to your friends and family at your funeral, exactly as you would like to be remembered.
7. What one change could you make in your behavior today that would help you to live in greater harmony with your values?

About Brian

Brian Tracy is one of the top business experts and trainers in the world. He has taught more than 5,000,000 sales people in 80 countries.

He is the President of Brian Tracy International, committed to teaching ambitious individuals how to rapidly increase their sales and personal incomes.

CHAPTER 2

SALES SECRETS OF THE SHY AND INTROVERTED
A ROADMAP FOR THOSE OF US WHO CAN'T STAND SELLING

BY JASON MINION

I was an introvert growing up. Not just shy, but an intense introvert. My fear of rejection was paralyzing at times, and I lived in a near-perpetual state of guilt—not because I had done anything wrong, but because I was afraid that at any moment someone might come along and *tell* me I had.

But like everyone, I had dreams. I longed for more. I wanted to create success in my life, but at the same time, I struggled with an intense fear of the attention that might come with achieving more.

In an attempt to find a way through this dilemma, I became a perfectionist. The best way to avoid criticism, I reasoned, was simply to never make any mistakes at all. That, of course, failed. Instead, my unrealistic perfectionism made me feel worthless and undeserving of success.

Over time, I rationalized my less-than-ideal life. I built a compelling list of reasons why it was safer for me to remain guarded and fly under the radar. *Keep your head down,* I told myself, *and let the extroverts do the talking.*

That approach got me through the day, but it didn't help me build a life.

THE ACCIDENTAL SALESMAN

I landed in sales by accident and immediately found myself deeply conflicted. I loved the industry, but hated the thought of selling. I believed in our products, but had no faith in myself. While I knew what we offered could change everyone for the better, sales felt like just another word for *manipulation*. I couldn't bring myself to use sales 'tactics' on others. Just the thought of words like 'prospect' and 'closer' made me nauseous.

It was no surprise when, after the first year, I finished at the bottom of the sales team. It was also no surprise that my job was on the chopping block. I was broke, unhappy, and about to be fired.

In desperation, I began to look for ways I could find success in sales without changing who I was. *Surely, I thought, there's a way for people like me to succeed in sales and life.*

It turns out that there is.

RETHINKING SALES

If you classify yourself as reserved, even introverted, or you feel that sales is somehow a profession tainted with more than a little inauthenticity, you're being held captive by a mistaken belief.

Believe me, I faced the same challenge. Before I discovered a new approach to selling, I believed sales was a *performance*—a sort of three-ring circus made up of misdirection, false enthusiasm, and psychological trickery.

That belief not only kept me from thriving in an industry that I loved, but it kept me from seeing that what I thought was holding me back—my introversion—was in fact, my superpower for success. It also kept me from realizing that we *all* sell, even if we don't carry the title of salesperson. In all our roles, professional and personal, we need to be able to effectively connect the dots between what we have, and what others want.

At the time, I didn't understand any of this. All I knew was that if I didn't figure out how to sell, I was going to lose my job. And so, reluctantly accepting that a little sales savvy might go a long way to improving my potential for success in *any* profession, I set out to learn what I could. With my livelihood on the line, I began to dig into everything available about sales, hoping I might find a way forward that didn't compromise my integrity.

What I found changed more than my outlook on sales; it changed my whole life. I found that not only can sales be as authentic, enjoyable and giving as any profession, but that introverts and other "non-salespeople" have many natural advantages that make them exceptional at the job.

Armed with my new knowledge, I set out to put it to the test. It wasn't long before I discovered, to my surprise, that I was good at sales. Better than good. I was *great*. Within months I climbed from the bottom rung of the sales team. Within a few years, I was Sales Director for an entire company.

And it was all thanks to the very thing that I'd always felt was holding me back.

THE FIVE STEPS ON YOUR SALES JOURNEY

The turning point in my sales career came when I learned to

reframe the job of "salesperson" from a misplaced stereotype, to a repeatable process that leveraged my strengths as an introvert. After some experimentation, I built a five-step roadmap that not only delivered plenty of sales, but delighted customers, creating a virtuous cycle of success that took me from the chopping block to the top of the company.

The steps form a conversational *map*, one that guides you through five necessary waypoints on a journey to sales success. Each step is critical, as is the order in which you reach them; missing a step or applying the steps out of order can derail your journey. Fortunately, the steps are easy to remember and flow naturally from one to the next.

The best part is that this journey is designed for *you and me*—for the introverts... for the shy... for the people who want to feel authentic, and who want to help... for those who want to use their natural talents to bring the two things to sales that we all so desperately need: a sense of authenticity and a feeling of success.

STEP 1: Bring Yourself

A common reason for introverts to dislike sales is that it feels like acting. Sales feels like a performance where you play the part of someone who isn't you. The problem with that feeling is that it stops us cold before we even begin.

Sales starts with the greeting, and this is where we begin to change the script with one simple idea: stop acting. You don't like being someone you're not, and neither do customers— they can tell from the moment you reach out your hand.

Remember that for many customers, entering into a sales process feels just as uncomfortable for them as it does for you. So be yourself. Think about how you would appreciate being welcomed into a conversation, and just do that.

The takeaway: <u>Be authentic</u>. The salesperson who puts customers most at ease earns the right to build a connection.

STEP 2: Seek the Truth

Dr. Steven Covey said, "Seek first to understand, then to be understood." This isn't just great interpersonal advice, it's a gift to anyone who struggles with the role of salesperson.

It's time to reframe the role and leave the circus. Rather than a performer or seller, think of yourself as a counselor, or a detective. Your new job isn't to sell, it's to *discover*. And what you're seeking is how you can best help the person standing right in front of you.

That's a job that introverts excel at. We're great listeners and naturally curious about others. Forget about what you're supposed to *sell*—instead, use your listening superpower to unearth the problem that the person in front of you needs to *solve*.

The magic of this step is that it turns the traditional idea of sales on its head. Rather than jumping into your offering, focus on the customer. Do what you do best: learn about *them*.

The takeaway: <u>Go slowly</u>. It's not about you. The salesperson who does the best job of making the customer feel understood, earns the right to go one step further on the journey to winning their business. Be that person.

STEP 3: Become the Teacher

Introverts are natural connectors. We may not always be outspoken, but we have an innate drive for closer connection. And that makes us ideally suited for this third stop on our conversational journey.

Customers often arrive armed with their own research and a long list of online reviews. But if that were enough, they would have already bought what they needed. Instead, they've found themselves flush with information, but short on *insight*. That's where you come in. This is your opportunity to use your natural aptitude for education.

As introverts, our drive for meaningful connection means we can educate our customers far better than most. Where the typical salesperson might *talk* in a one-way stream of product information, your approach should be to *teach*. It's a natural fit for your style and an excellent sales tool.

Now is your chance to prove why it's not just your product or service that is best for the needs you've identified, but also why *you* are as well. The easiest way is to take the time to educate your customers and add insight to the information they almost certainly already have.

The takeaway: Don't tell; teach. The salesperson who provides the best education, aligned with their customer's needs, instills the highest level of confidence.

STEP 4: Offer an Answer

You've done your best to make your customer feel understood. You've worked to increase your customer's confidence in their decision to invest with you by first investing in them through education. Now you need to take the next step: providing a "WOW!" experience in demonstrating what you offer.

For many introverts, this can feel troublesome. Don't be fooled; "WOW!" doesn't mean flashy or loud. What really wows customers is someone who shows them an *answer*—the perfect solution to the problem uncovered in Step 3. Give the customer an experience that ties back to their reasons for wanting to buy. This could be a goal-specific feature, or testimonials that support the education you provided in the previous step. It could be evidence to show the ROI provided by your offering.

Whatever you do, don't forget the previous steps. Your job isn't to demonstrate what *you* like about the product, it's to demonstrate how well it solves *their* challenge.

The takeaway: Demonstrate a *solution*. The salesperson who does the best to provide an aligned WOW! factor with their offering reaps the benefit of getting another step closer to "Yes!"

STEP 5: Enable Yes

I'm not a big fan of the term 'close.' As a customer, I certainly don't want to be closed any more than I want to be 'sold to.' Still, no conversation is a sale until a customer says yes. But rather than using a dozen different tactics to convince a customer to say yes, your job is to ensure that you've made yes *possible*—that you've enabled it by discovering their problem, educating them on the options, and demonstrating a fitting solution.

Put yourself in your customer's shoes: would you appreciate an uncomfortable 'ask' that puts you on your heels? Not likely, and in most cases, it only creates resistance.

Respect the customer's right to choose. Make sure you've done enough in Steps 1 through 4 so that the only question left to answer for the customer is "How soon can I have it?"

The takeaway: Think of yourself as a tour guide working to provide your customer with the very best experience that doesn't just encourage positive feedback, but inspires it.

STOP SELLING AND START CONNECTING

I believe that introverts are natural relationship builders. We tune in to others. We like to listen more than talk. We're sensitive to the needs of those around us and have an inherent desire to help. It makes us ideally suited to connect with customers, to uncover their needs, and to match them with the perfect solution.

Where our natures don't serve us is in a conventional sales approach—the kind of zero-sum, us-versus-them mindset where only one person can emerge victorious.

So stop *selling*. Your customer conversations aren't a competitive chess match. Rather than trying to sell your customer, make it your intention to *help them buy*. They are two very different things, and the person who does the latter best makes the transition from salesperson to the coveted title of *trusted advisor*.

Common wisdom has always been that you need to believe in what you're selling to succeed. But for introverts like us? We need something even more fundamental. We need to believe in *ourselves*.

About Jason

Jason Minion is a sales coach who helps reserved and introverted professionals thrive in a world where selling and marketing have become a part of every job.

Surprisingly, Jason is a self-declared introvert as well, and started out as anything but a salesperson. He believed he worked best behind the scenes, supporting the "real" sellers of the world. But when his love of fitness inadvertently landed him in a sales position, he found himself well out of his comfort zone and struggling to stay afloat. It wasn't long before Jason was faced with a difficult choice: learn to sell or lose his job.

It was a tough spot. Everything Jason knew about sales felt manipulative and deceitful. The sales approaches he was taught were rigid, filled with scripts and uncomfortable techniques. Sales, as Jason knew it, wasn't much fun for customers *or* salespeople. And it certainly wasn't a fit for introverts who would rather do almost *anything* but sell.

Still, Jason was determined to embrace sales and find an approach that honored both the customer *and* the salesperson. More than anything, he wanted to find a way for people like him to remain authentic in their work.

Jason's quest, like that of many salespeople, took him through a seemingly endless stream of books, coaches, and training programs. None of the traditional approaches seemed to fit, and with nowhere left to turn, he started over. He created his own sales methodology built not on tactics or contrived scripts, but on a simple, conversational map that felt *right*. Best of all, it did the one thing every salesperson wants: it enabled prospective clients to easily say *yes*.

It wasn't long before he began to see results. Instead of being fired, Jason was promoted, ...then promoted again. Soon he was running the retail operations for the entire company.

Since creating that first "conversation map," Jason has transformed himself from a struggling salesperson on the brink of losing his job to a C-suite executive leading an entire sales team—all of whom have been trained using the same sales methodology that Jason designed.

Along the way, he's discovered that selling isn't what he thought it was. It doesn't have to feel forced or manipulative. And it most certainly is *not* just for the extroverts of the world.

Now, Jason brings his unique sales approach to companies around the world, helping sales teams and executives—and especially introverts—reach their potential in sales while remaining authentic.

To learn more about "Enabling Yes", and Jason's unique sales training methodology, visit:

- www.JasonMinion.com
- linkedin.com/in/jasonminion
- instagram.com/jasonjminion
- facebook.com/jasonjminion

CHAPTER 3

FROM A YELLOW DUCK TO A WHITE SWAN

BY MINA VO

What if you know that you can tap into your potential with a snap of your fingers and get what you want in life? What if I tell you that whatever you want, you can have and achieve it? You would say: *"Yeah, yeah right, what are you trying to tell me?"* To be honest, I did not know about the Law of Attraction until a year ago and I can tell you, it changed my life drastically since. I now have more time with my family, I became a co-author in this book with Brian Tracy which I couldn't ever have imagined that I could, and most of all, I have become a better person for myself and my loved ones – a person that I dreamed to be – and I know that the best is yet to come! I hope that you will gain some insight by reading this book and learning from all of us in order to get what you want in life, and make your dreams come true.

As far as dreaming is concerned, I'm overwhelmed with my dreams. I come from a very modest family. Being an immigrant to Canada on August 1st, 1980, everything was new for me at that time – the snow, the culture, friends, and the environment. At thirteen years old, I spoke neither English nor French. Because of the language barrier, they put me in Grade 4 in a French school in Quebec instead of Grade 8, as I was in, back in Vietnam. I wasn't happy, but I had to accept it, because the only word I knew in French was, "Merci".

Gratitude is always by my side. My family and I are very fortunate to be able to come to this beautiful country. Back then, I was a very shy girl, not even able to ask for anything. I remember exactly that time in school when they were giving out milk to students in elementary school every morning. On that first day at school, my teacher asked me if I wanted a carton of milk, "Mina, veux-tu un berlingot de lait?" I would have liked to have one, but instead of saying "Oui", I intentionally said, "Non, Merci". But, deep down inside of me, I really wanted to have one, just to tell you how shy I was... So, for the rest of the school year, I didn't have a drop of milk while my friends were savoring theirs. I missed my first opportunity in one of the lands of plenty, my second homeland, Canada.

When I was 28, Canada was now a part of me. I integrated well into the North American culture, so with my B.Sc. in Biology on hand, I officially entered the work force and started to reassert myself. The idea of *"who cares what people think about me"* invaded my mindset. I felt free to be able to choose the husband I wanted and moved out of my parents' house, 160 miles away from home. We built our family with three beautiful kids whom I adore, they are my inspiration!

After working as an employee for the government and a few private companies, from seamstress in a remote clothing shop to a research assistant, back and forth, with contracts here and there, I then had an urge to become an entrepreneur. So, I decided to start a food processing company. What an adventure it was! I've learned a lot from that experience and lost a lot too! Luckily, I have a wonderful husband who supported me all along the way, for better or worse. That experience has made me stronger as a woman, now I know how to assert myself, I'm not afraid to say "No" when it's time, and most of all, I can be myself. Sometimes people don't like it, but as long as I feel good about it, I'm attracting more and more happiness into my life, and that's all that counts.

I would say that even the stars were aligned in a way that you wouldn't even think they would be. The Law of Attraction just came to me at a moment I wasn't looking for it. I was searching something on the web, and somehow, Christy Whitman, founder and CEO of the Quantum Success Coaching Academy (QSCA) appeared on my screen. Until then, I had no idea what the Law of Attraction (LOA) was all about. Even when I decided to register for the course and got into it a few weeks later, I HAD NO IDEA WHAT THE LAW OF ATTRACTION WAS! I just wanted to become a life coach, and somehow, Christy Whitman gave me that feeling that she was authentic and a good teacher for me. Now, I am so glad that I've discovered the LOA. After a few checkups, I decided to follow my intuition and register for the QSCA program for a year (even though I had to load up my credit cards), because I no longer had passion for what I was doing at that time. I was looking for the next level.

I'm now a certified LOA Transformational Life Coach. I help people to transform and become a better person, to get what they want in life, to set goals and be disciplined to realize them. Helping my clients become *The Leader of their Life* is my ultimate goal. Watching them not only changing, but thriving to realize their dreams, fills my heart with love and compassion. To be able to change the life of one person at a time, so that they themselves can change the life of others, the torch is passed on. Then, I can say that my mission is accomplished on this planet Earth, which is: ***"To Influence and Inspire others to Achieve their Goals and Improve their lives in a Prosperous and Harmonious environment."***

Prosperity and Freedom are what we all wanted. There is something in this Law of Attraction that intrigues me. It is similar to the Law of Gravity, you don't notice it, but it's there. Anything you are thinking about, either negative or positive, you'll be attracted to it. The processes that I learned in the LOA have taught me to attract more of what I want, and I'm so glad that I have discovered it.

Most of the time, people don't get it. That's because they ask for something but don't believe they'll get it. The three secret ingredients in the LOA are simple: BELIEF, ACTION and DISCIPLINE. If any one of these is missing, then it will be hard for you to get what you want in life. My dream has always been to write books, and this has simmered in my mind for a long time.

When I received an e-mail from Nick Nanton from Celebrity Branding Agency inviting me to take a look at an opportunity to co-author a book with Brian Tracy, my heart told me that this is it! This is *The One Big Thing*! This is the moment I was waiting for! However, my head said, "Who am I to think about this move?" I was struggling between my decisions. You know, when your mind keeps telling you that, "Opportunity will come back next year and you'll have a chance to get it", then the 'other' mind said: "Opportunity comes and goes, and some of them might not come back". What should I do? Should I go for it? Or should I wait for the opportunity to come back again? What if it won't? Then I'm going to regret it for the rest of my life! Money I can find, but opportunity is rare, especially to co-author a book with someone like Brian Tracy. I still couldn't decide as yet, because the Universe had to send me a sign.

For three days, I asked God (Universe) to give me a sign to let me know that this *One Big Thing* book is destined for me.

Believe it or not, my first sign appeared from a YouTube video. There was a speech from Ulla Suokko (from a TEDx talk – I had no idea who she was before viewing this video). In that video, Ulla Suokko tells the audience about her story when she asked for a sign and she found it in a book. Is this a calling for me to write a book and inspire people so that I can help to influence and transform lives in this world? That startled me all day.

Then, when I went in to sleep that night, but before going to lie down, I asked God for a sign. Then, I had a dream that Sunday night. In my dream, I saw my deceased Mom; she was cleaning the kitchen in our house back in Vietnam in the country side, I remember that kitchen vividly, where Mom used to cook all our meals. Mom was cooking something that looked like debris of sorts, but it smelled really good! I asked her if she needed help, but she did not. Then, looking to my right, I saw a beautiful golden-brown kitten that was supposed to be a puppy from my dog (weird) that lay just under the table. I took the kitten and held it in my hands and looked at it and folded it into my arms. Then, a few seconds later, that golden-brown kitten was no longer brown, but it turned into a beautiful tiger with short white hair and stripes on its body.

I was surprised and woke up. Was the Universe trying to tell me that I could become whoever I wanted to become? I was a kitten and now I am a TIGER ready to get up and thrive? The decision was mine. I only had to decide and take ACTION! ... And really take MASSIVE ACTION. The decision to adhere to the program of Celebrity Branding was stirring in my head all the time during the next day. I knew that I had to make a decision, but somehow, I hesitated.

My hesitation led me once again to this third sign. I am a fan of Esther, Jerry and Abraham Hicks. Every morning in my car driving to work, I listen to a CD of *The Astonishing Power of Emotions* from Abraham Hicks. There is a passage in one of the CDs of that series in which Abraham made an observation, via Esther's translation, that triggered my decision to take action. It said: **"Wanting in Belief is Life Giving. Wanting in Doubt is Horrible!"**

After that profound moment listening and understanding, I said to myself, "That's it! I got it! Nothing can stop me now!" I shouldn't have any doubt if I want to change and go for the next level. It helped me to make a faster decision, and I was eager to come home that day on March 12th, 2019 to book into the program. That decision is the best one that I've ever made. Because of that "Action-Taking", I'm here now, ready for a change, and much, much more to come.

Change is never comfortable, it requires us to get out of our comfort zone. It requires more energy to adapt because change is unknown and it's sometimes scary. What's unknown to a human is uncomfortable. Unlike the animal species, we have the ability to be conscious of things we don't know. Most of the time, that consciousness prevents us from going forward, from taking action to go a step further, and striving for the next level. That's because we are afraid to fail, to be judged, to be ashamed or to be ridiculed. Isn't it because our ego is too big? We are not ready to be ready… and sometimes we say: "It's hard to be a human being!"

It's not easy, but it's simple. So simple that we make it complicated. Before letting you move on, I would like to pass on to you this phrase that I learned from Abraham Hicks and I repeat it every morning :

"God (Universe, Inner Being, etc.), I know that I'm the object of your positive attention and I appreciate your continual gaze on behalf of my well-being. And today, no matter where I am, no matter where I'm going, no matter what I'm doing and no matter who I'm doing it with, I'll be in conscious awareness that YOU TOO are there with me – Guiding me, Teaching me, Inspiring me, Acknowledging me, Supporting me, Showing me the way, Helping me, Inspiring me, and Having fun with me… Thank you for everything you've done for me until now and to the end of my existence on this marvelous planet earth."

My practice specializes in helping professional women who want to transform to have more freedom of choices, and through the years of experience, I'm confident that no problem is too great to overcome. Through coaching, there is always a way to address the issues you face and to learn coping strategies to help you to become the person you dream to be right now and in the future.

About Mina

Mina Vo is a Law of Attraction Transformational Life Coach who specializes in Personal Growth, Self Confidence, Leadership and Career Transformation coaching, and she maintains a private practice online.

Mina is the Founder of Mina Vo Coaching and Co-founder of Nail Tech Expert. She serves as a private practitioner working with a broad spectrum of clients, especially professional women. In addition to being a professional Life Coach, she also presented nationally to general audiences speaking on the topic of GOAL SETTING and CAREER ADAPTATION by using The Law of Attraction concepts and processes.

Mina is a collaborative, solution-focused Life Coach. Through this approach, she provides support and practical feedback to help clients effectively address personal life challenges. She also integrates coaching techniques and helpful assignments to offer highly-personalized programs tailored to you. With compassion and understanding, she works with you to help build on your strengths and attain the personal growth you are committed to achieving.

Seeing her clients' evolution, their mindset change and their personal growth expanding to be better themselves and take ACTIONS to become THE LEADERS OF THEIR LIVES, make her feel blessed. With this passionate choice to become a life coach, she's now having more time with her family, doing things that she loves whenever and wherever that suits her.

Knowing that her work can help someone who might influence others to become better with their positive attitude and mindset, to become more conscious about their strengths and weaknesses so that they can help themselves and other around them to live harmoniously with each other, she can then say: "My mission is accomplished."

Mina's Mission:

"To Influence and Inspire others to Achieve their Goals and Improve their lives in a Prosperous and Harmonious environment."

To connect with Mina :

- www.minavocoaching.com
- info@minavocoaching.com
- Facebook: https://www.facebook.com/minavocoaching/
- Instagram: https://www.instagram.com/mina__vo
- LinkedIn: http://linkedin.com/in/mina-vo-455074139
- Twitter: https://www.twitter.com/minavo1/
- Website: www.nailtechexpert.com

To learn more about becoming a certified QSCA coach :

- https://christywhitman.isrefer.com/go/qscavideos/MinaVo/

CHAPTER 4

FOUR CRITICAL MARKETING MISTAKES THAT ARE DESTROYING YOUR PROFITS

BY GREG ROLLETT

I am going to warn you in advance: This isn't going to be easy… or pretty.

What follows is bound to serve as a wake-up call for business owners—especially if you spend your time waiting, hoping and praying for the phone to ring with new orders. That is no way to run a business. If no one is calling, stopping in, emailing you, or visiting your website, then it may be your fault that business is stagnant.

"…But Greg, my *business* is different."

I hear this all the time. When I hear a version of, "…but my business is different," I counter with, "Does your business involve working with people?"

At the end of the day, someone has to sign off on a purchase order, hand over a credit card, or sign an authorization form. The fundamental fact is that if there's a person on the other end of that transaction, then your business isn't different.

You see, people buy people. More specifically, they buy from people they know, like, and trust.

So, while you are sitting at your desk today, waiting for the phone to ring, I'm going to outline the four biggest mistakes you are making with your marketing that are both costing you money and may be the root reason why nothing is coming back in.

Look, I want you to be booked from the minute that you get into the office until you leave. But, I only want your schedule to be full of qualified people who know you, like you and trust you—ultimately making them ready and willing to do business with you. And these four mistakes are holding you back from the goldmine of clients eagerly waiting to do business with you.

MISTAKE #1: YOU SEE YOURSELF AS A DOER AND NOT A MARKETER...

Your first mistake is failing to see the significance of marketing your business, thinking clients will just show up.

I bet you are not providing goods or services out of the kindness of your heart. Sure, we are in business to help people, but let's be real: we're in business to make profits and provide our family and ourselves with a better life.

If you're in business for any reason that involves your financial wellbeing, then you must see yourself as a marketer of the services that you provide. You must get your mind off the idea that you are in a particular business and accept that you are instead, a marketer of the services you provide.

If you own a dental practice, you are not in the dental business.

You are in the business of marketing your dental services to your market. Let's say you are the best technical dentist in the world, yet your chair is always empty. Does it matter how good a dentist you are if you have no patients to help?

It's the same thing if you are a financial advisor or a real estate agent. You are really in the business of marketing financial services or real estate services.

When it comes to marketing, you should think in terms of marketing systems. Systems are what make things work with purpose rather than the result of happenstance. If you're waiting, hoping and praying for your phone to ring, or someone to walk through the door, you don't have a system in place. And the best type of marketing system is a trust-based marketing system – a system that continues to develop relationships with your market, engaging them and allowing them to know you, like you and trust you.

Without a trust-based marketing system, you can't have predictable income or revenue. You won't have a client list that is constantly being attracted to your business and is bankable every month. That's what a trust-based marketing system does. It greases the gears of your business.

But, let's not put the cart before the horse. Having a system is just part of the battle. Winning the war for your prospects' attention and money is impossible if you are "just another business."

MISTAKE #2: YOU AREN'T POSITIONING YOURSELF AS IMPORTANT TO YOUR MARKET…

Mistake number two is about stature. If your prospects just throw you into a category with everyone else "in the business of whatever you do", then you have no competitive advantage. When there is no competitive advantage, price becomes your only ammunition against the other guys.

If you are competing on price—you are losing the war, one eroding sale at a time.

Who wants to compete on price? There is always someone who "will do it" for less, whatever "it" is. It is a terrible way to do business. You don't want to be the $19.99 oil change shop and suddenly you've got to do an $18.99 oil change, because the guy next door reduced his price.

Price should not be the reason for customers to come to you. You need to have a reason for people to do business with you, and it's generally deeper than just the features and benefits of your products or services.

It starts by creating perceived importance. Money flows to those perceived as important.

Quick: Why do celebrities, athletes, and entertainers make more money than most people? *Because we perceive them to have more importance and stature.*

Whether you're a sales professional, in private practice, or in any other business, you need to be more important than the competition in your marketplace.

"Greg, how can I be seen as important?"

It's actually rather simple. Start talking about and doing things that are important to your marketplace. Start with media. People that are seen in the media are important. A columnist for a major newspaper is perceived to be more important than the guy who is just blogging for fun on the weekends.

Start being seen around important people and at important events. And show off your importance in your own media. In your monthly print newsletters and in marketing promotions sent to your prospects and clients. If you never tell anyone you were on TV or on the radio or met someone perceived as important, how are they ever going to know and thus raise your importance in their eyes?

The bottom line: If you are doing what everyone else does, you'll get lumped in with everyone else. That is going to keep your phones silent, your balance sheet out of whack, and keep you broke.

MISTAKE #3: YOU DON'T UNDERSTAND WHO YOUR MARKET IS, AND INSTEAD, YOU TRY TO BE "ALL THINGS TO ALL PEOPLE"...

Mistake number three is a fundamental flaw that plagues nearly every business owner at some point. If you don't actually understand who your market is, then you can't properly attract them to your business. When you do that, you fail.

People pay more for absolutes. Money flows to business owners who have absolute opinions of authority. Media personalities like Sean Hannity, Glenn Beck, Howard Stern, Dave Ramsey and Rush Limbaugh have very specific topics for which they have very specific opinions of authority. While many of their viewpoints can be controversial, their absolute opinions raise their celebrity—and their profits.

People won't pay top dollar for wishy-washy answers or flip-flopping.

If every time someone asked me a marketing question, I gave a general answer, I'd be out of business. Though often the correct answer is something like this:

"It depends and we should test it."

THE ONE BIG THING

That's not what people pay me for. When someone calls in with a question I need to give them an absolute answer:

- "Make this offer."
- "This strategy will work for you."
- "Run with this headline."

Think about it, if you went to a financial adviser with $500,000 to start planning for retirement, wouldn't you want him to tell you exactly what to do? If he waffles on the clear path to your retirement success, why should you trust him with your money?

Would you feel secure if your doctor started second guessing his diagnosis? You sure wouldn't. This is why you need to form strong opinions of authority and solve specific problems for specific markets. People want specialists with specific skill sets.

I just had a new baby, so I'm consistently in need of something for the little one. If I need sage advice on products for my child, what are my options?

I could go to a generalist, like Wal-Mart. Wal-Mart serves everything to everyone. Odds are the guy stocking the shelves in the baby section is the same guy stocking the groceries or electronics. If I needed milk AND potting soil AND baby clothes, then maybe I'd seek them out.

Continuing with the baby analogy, specialty stores like Babies "R" Us, or Buy Buy Baby at least have some people trained to know about babies and baby products. It's a step in the right direction for a customer, but the odds are slim of finding an expert who can tailor a specific solution for your problem when the guy stocking the shelves is probably still slightly above minimum wage.

So, what's the "next level specialist?" Can I find the guy who hosts a TV show, or is the go-to source for the media when it comes to baby safety? Maybe he wrote a Best-Selling book on baby safety. I could hire the guy that's on TV talking about babies and baby safety, bring him into my specific home and scenario, and he can actually do the work for me.

If I find that guy, he is getting paid a whole heck of a lot more that the guy at Wal-Mart. In your business, that is what you want to be, but you have to be a specialist for a certain market. You can't be a generalist. In order to be seen as a specialist, you must create marketing that positions you that way, to a very specific and targeted market.

If you've fixed the first three mistakes, you are heading towards a business boom, but there is one final pratfall to avoid on the way to the big time!

MISTAKE #4: YOU'RE NOT MAKING ENOUGH OFFERS...

The fourth and final mistake sounds simple, but you'd be surprised at how many business owners are making this mistake. You're not selling enough.

"But Greg, I'm on the phone selling all day."

That's not what I mean. I mean you're not making enough offers to the marketplace to give you an opportunity to sell. Your income is directly proportional to the number of offers you send into your marketplace. So, if you're not out there presenting your services, sending out offers, and pre-converting prospects to clients, then there is no way that people can do business with you.

It isn't magic or witchcraft, nor does it occur by happenstance. It means spending money on media, advertising, and aggressively going out and marketing your business.

It doesn't mean sitting in your room in your underwear writing blog posts. It doesn't mean that you tweet or post to Pinterest.

It means that you're out there making a direct solicitation to do business with someone by saying,

"Hey, you have this problem. I can solve it. Here's how I can help you."

If you're not making offers, you're going to continue to NOT make the money that you desire from your business. You're not going to have the profits and you're not going to have the lifestyle that you wanted when you got into business for yourself.

People aren't just going to show up consistently. This isn't *Field of Dreams*. They don't come just because you built it. They come because they responded to an offer.

Send something to your prospects right now, I'll wait. Tell them about a new product or service. Go to all your prospects that you haven't converted and ask them to do business with you by demonstrating your expertise. Send them an email: "Hey, you want to do some business?" It might sound crazy, but someone's going to say yes.

Ok, I'm aware of everything I'm doing wrong in my marketing, how can I fix it and start making more money?

It all starts by seeing yourself as a marketer and not just a dentist or a financial advisor or a real estate agent. Position yourself as a trusted resource and advisor who solves people's problems.

If your perceived importance is lacking, then work on building your clout in the market. Address a specific market, add value to their lives and then directly solicit them. When they read a piece of mail that comes from you, or see an ad in the newspaper or your website, make sure they know you are speaking directly to them. Get them to know you, like you and trust you.

For example, let's say you are a financial advisor who does dinner seminars. Instead of inviting people to come eat a free steak, which is the same thing everyone else in your niche does, create perceived importance by saying:

"Best-Selling Author reveals his eight keys to success based on his Best-Selling Book. He's also been seen in The Wall Street Journal, as well as ABC, NBC, CBS and Fox affiliates."

Do you see how this fundamentally changes your position from one of sameness to one of authority?

We're all in the business of marketing. We're all in the business of sales. It doesn't matter what you do or what products you sell. Your business is not different. It's very important for you to understand that, if nothing else here today.

Your ability to market your business is the driving factor behind how much money you take home. That money is being able to keep the lights on, pay your employees, and take that vacation. That money is being able to create the lifestyle that you wanted from your business.

Isn't is time you started acting like a marketer?

About Greg

Greg is an Emmy® Award-Winning Producer, Best-Selling Author and Marketing Expert who works with experts, authors and entrepreneurs all over the world. He utilizes the power of new media, direct response and personality-driven marketing to attract more clients and to create more freedom in the businesses and lives of his clients.

After creating a successful string of his own educational products and businesses, Greg began helping others in the production and marketing of their own products and services.

Greg has written for *Mashable, Fast Company, Inc.com, The Huffington Post, AOL, AMEX's OPEN Forum* and others, and continues to share his message helping experts and entrepreneurs grow their business through marketing. He has co-authored best-selling books with Jack Canfield, Dan Kennedy, Brian Tracy, Tom Hopkins, James Malinchak, Robert Allen, Ryan Lee and many other leading experts from around the world.

Greg's client list includes Michael Gerber, Brian Tracy, Tom Hopkins, Sally Hogshead, Coca-Cola, Miller Lite and Warner Brothers, along with thousands of entrepreneurs and small-business owners across the world. Greg's work has been featured on FOX News, ABC, NBC, CBS, CNN, *USA Today, Inc. Magazine, Fast Company, The Wall Street Journal, The Daily Buzz* and more.

To contact Greg, please visit:
- http://ambitious.com
- greg@ambitious.com

CHAPTER 5

THE STATE OF YOUR SEO: TAKE A MINUTE AND TAKE STOCK

BY LINDSAY DICKS

Sometimes, when our website is humming along, seemingly doing everything it's meant and supposed to do, we fall into the "set-it-and-forget-it" mindset. In other words, we figure, "If it ain't broke, don't fix it."

Until it is. Broken, that is. Suddenly, something goes wrong. Maybe pages that looked great don't display right? Perhaps you stop getting contact form completions? Or distressingly, you are no longer ranking in Google for terms you used to dominate?

In any case, for some reason or other, it quickly becomes clear—you should have been paying more attention to your website all along.

The moral of the story should be clear…

Don't ever get complacent with the state of your site. The risks are too great. Wise 'webionados' do this. Don't you want to be a wise webionado too?

Let's talk about how to join that group—the smart website owners who frequently take stock of their website, its effectiveness and efficiency as well as its visibility. And, who also course correct when they expect it might be needed soon, but before it really becomes an emergency.

I.   Website Design Review

Some website design trends can change on a dime. Web design best practices, however, stay pretty constant.

In general, if you want or need to get by with making design tweaks and alterations as seldom as possible, keeping it simple is usually the best option. Clean, minimal-special-effect and notoverly- designed sites carry many benefits. It's easy to sometimes think we need a lot of cool features, brilliant copy and a ton of text to have a "great" website. Yet, in most cases, less is truly 'more.'

One good thing about a minimalistic website design is that it forces you to really dial in to what you want – and need – to say, to attract and convert leads. It gets right to the point, maximizing and respecting your prospects' precious time (an average time on site for STRONG websites is two minutes!).

Another is that there is less that can 'go wrong' with design. If you focus on crisp visuals and value-driven content, you rarely go wrong.

According to Website Magazine[1] – here are what their experts consider the five biggest benefits of simple websites:
1. Simple websites convert better.
2. Simple web designs load faster.
3. Simple designs are more mobile-friendly.
4. Simple websites cost less.
5. Simple websites reduce user friction.

---
1. https://www.websitemagazine.com/blog/the-undeniable-benefits-ofsimple-website-design

II. Conversion Testing and Optimization

When it comes to conversion, what 'works' stays fairly constant, but there is almost always room for improvement.

As with most things, the conversion ratios you experience in the beginning—or when you first start working on the conversion process—seem fantastic! Then, over time, you yearn for 'more' and 'better.' When you start to feel that way, be sure not to throw the baby out with the bath water. In other words, don't just assume that something is 'wrong' and you need to trash everything and start over.

Instead, you should consider what you can test and improve to make your conversion numbers better. Some of the things to test – usually utilizing a specific type of web conversion analysis and optimization called "A/B Testing." This is where you will test one change against a constant. Another is called "multivariate testing" – where you will test multiple elements of your conversion process.

Here are some factors of your website you might consider examining and where you might try to improve conversion:

- Landing page or page / post titles
- Landing page or page / post headlines and sub-headlines
- Colors (of titles, headlines and other elements)
- Fonts
- Copy
- Calls-to-action
- The text on submission buttons
- Fields you are requesting be completed on forms
- Where forms are positioned on a page
- Upsells, cross-sells and one-time offers

III. SEO: Performing a Website Audit

Don't wait for your rank to take a tumble—or start to decline—

before checking the state of your search engine optimization. There are many tools out there that can help you perform a thorough website SEO audit and they make it quick, easy and painless.

The tools to assist you in performing a full and comprehensive website audit can, however, be a little pricey. Thus, you might want to check and see if your website provider, web designer or SEO firm offers such a service. This also gives you the added benefit of usually having someone there who can help you fix or correct any issues that might be found.

Here are some things a good website SEO audit will take a look at:

- If your URLS are "clean"
- Whether there is a Robots.txt file present and configured correctly
- If your site has an XML site map and it's been submitted to the search engines
- That the site does not use flash or frames
- If meta titles and descriptions are present and not duplicated
- If heading tags are present and utilized properly
- If the site is Open Auth compliant
- If structured data and schema are present and correctly identified
- If the site is AMP ready
- If knowledge graph data is present and written right
- Whether all images have correct titles and alt tags
- The status of internal and outbound links, as well as the links coming in to the site (inbound links)
- Whether inbound and external links have optimized anchor text
- That content is keyword rich but not overly spammy
- Server response time
- The presence and importance of any 404 (page not found) errors
- Whether code is clean and minimized where possible

THE STATE OF YOUR SEO: TAKE A MINUTE AND TAKE STOCK

- If the site passes W3C HTML validation

While you obviously can't predict or foresee everything that might go wrong with your website, the ideas and tips above should at least help you be protected and prepared. Ultimately, that's the best you can do – for yourself and for the health of your business. For those whose business depends on website health, this is especially critical. And it's really too simple to not address upfront, in advance.

About Lindsay

Lindsay Dicks helps her clients tell their stories in the online world. Being brought up around a family of marketers, but a product of Generation Y, Lindsay naturally gravitated to the new world of on-line marketing. Lindsay began freelance writing in 2000 and soon after launched her own PR firm that thrived by offering an in-your-face "Guaranteed PR" that was one of the first of its type in the nation.

Lindsay's new media career is centered on her philosophy that "people buy people." Her goal is to help her clients build a relationship with their prospects and customers. Once that relationship is built and they learn to trust them as the expert in their field, then they will do business with them. Lindsay also built a proprietary process that utilizes social media marketing, content marketing and search engine optimization to create online "buzz" for her clients that helps them to convey their business and personal story. Lindsay's clientele spans the entire business map and ranges from doctors and small business owners to Inc. 500 CEOs.

Lindsay is a graduate of the University of Florida. She is the CEO of CelebritySites™, an online marketing company specializing in social media and online personal branding. Lindsay is recognized as one of the top online marketing experts in the world, and has co-authored more than 25 best-selling books alongside authors such as Steve Forbes, Richard Branson, Brian Tracy, Jack Canfield (creator of the *Chicken Soup for the Soul* series), Dan Kennedy, Robert Allen, Dr. Ivan Misner (founder of BNI), Jay Conrad Levinson (author of the *Guerilla Marketing* series), Leigh Steinberg and many others, including the breakthrough hit, *Celebrity Branding You!*

She has also been selected as one of America's PremierExperts™ and has been quoted in *Forbes, Newsweek, The Wall Street Journal, USA Today,* and *Inc.* magazine as well as featured on NBC, ABC, and CBS television affiliates – speaking on social media, search engine optimization and making more money online. Lindsay was also brought on FOX 35 News as their Online Marketing Expert.

Lindsay, a national speaker, has shared the stage with some of the top speakers in the world, including Brian Tracy, Lee Milteer, Ron LeGrand,

Arielle Ford, Leigh Steinberg, Dr. Nido Qubein, Dan Sullivan, David Bullock, Peter Shankman and many others. Lindsay was also a Producer on the Emmy-winning film, *Jacob's Turn*, and sits on the advisory board for the Global Economic Initiative.

You can connect with Lindsay at:

- Lindsay@CelebritySites.com
- www.twitter.com/LindsayMDicks
- www.facebook.com/LindsayDicks

CHAPTER 6

CHECK YOUR TICKET TO FINANCIAL FREEDOM

BY DEBBIE NEUMAYER

Let's admit it. Most of us dream of making huge sums of money, since our "wants" always exceed the restrictions of a regular paycheck. For a multitude of reasons, extra income is always welcomed! To meet this burgeoning need, today's entrepreneurs embrace side hustles, such as renting out rooms in their homes, driving people around in rideshare enterprises, walking pets, and many other gigs.

Long before the side hustle economy became popular, I was a single mom of two children, engaged in gigs of my own. By day, I was employed as a copywriter. On the side, I authored natural health-topic booklets for a small publishing house and was paid a stipend for each one. I also created job-targeted resumes for clients, where I matched their qualifications to the positions they were interested in.

Since I began doing this in the pre-Internet 1980s, I advertised my services in the local newspaper with the tagline "Get a Better Job with a Better Resume." I would interview clients by phone and then create their resumes on my home computer. They would come to the house to review the draft and, at that point, I would make any changes and laser print a new version and they would then pay me for the resume.

This extra income helped with my budget, but to make more, I had to do more. Side hustles are a flexible way to bring in extra money. However, when the gig is over, the money stops and you have to start all over again. And again. And again.

Even though I believe a stable job is a real blessing, I needed to find something I could do to create a passive income flow—money that I could earn even when I was on vacation. Financial freedom was going to be The One Big Thing for me. Successful artists, musicians, and authors create a product once and then reap royalties on a repeat basis. Inventors do the same thing. However, was there a way the average person could make this type of income happen?

Oil magnate and billionaire J. Paul Getty is quoted as saying:

> *If you want to be financially independent,*
> *you have to do three things:*
> *(1) Be in business for yourself.*
> *(2) Have a product people need and want.*
> *(3) Be able to duplicate.*

In my research, I discovered that the business model of network marketing fulfills all three objectives. Ironically, I had been serving as a copywriter in that field for my working career. However, I had been cocooned as an in-house salaried employee, writing advertising and marketing content, not out in the trenches, so to speak. Sometimes marketers out in the field would visit the home office and I was impressed at their energy and how easily they spoke with all kinds of people. I knew that many of these go-getters were top earners, garnering six and seven-figure incomes. However, as a salaried writer I was concentrating on my own little world, so I didn't pay much attention to that fact at the time.

My research revealed that network marketing works along the same three-pronged premise described by J. Paul Getty: (1) It offers a business opportunity to people from all walks of life, at a low investment cost. (2) It's built on marketing products that people need and want. (3) The business model, much like franchising, is created on the principle of duplication.

Network marketing is all about building a network of people who buy and use a product of value. The company shares a portion of profit on each product sale with those who help other customers get started on these products. It's a profit-sharing model in its finest form! I like the idea of multiplying my efforts through unlimited numbers of people and helping others reach financial freedom by doing the same thing.

Working together as a team increases everyone's bonuses, commissions, and profits many-fold. If I train my people how to duplicate my efforts, each member can make a commission from each and every product sold through their individual "business center." You can tell the quality of products by the ratio of customers to business builders. In my particular company, about 85 percent of the people are just taking the product every month and not participating in the compensation plan. This makes it a very sustainable business model.

Some people dabble in network marketing as a hobby, but I've learned if you treat it like a business, it will pay you like a business. Network marketing is not a "get rich quick" scheme. Many entrepreneurial enterprises take an average of five years to break even from an initial investment. Network marketing professionals take an average of five years to build six-and seven-figure incomes. However, many accomplish this benchmark even sooner.

NETWORK MARKETING MAKES BUSINESS SENSE

Network marketing is a cost-effective way to bring a product to market. Instead of spending millions via traditional advertising venues or channeling products through hiring brokers and retailers, network marketing companies pay their "distributors" commissions and bonuses resulting from word-of-mouth or online advertising. On the flip side, the independent reps don't have to worry about inventorying products, handling sales, or shipping: the company does everything for them! All they need to do is share information.

The network marketing business model offers an equal opportunity to everyone. It doesn't restrict you based on age, income, educational background, work experience or any other parameter. Millennials to baby boomers, and everyone in between, can reap the benefits of their network marketing efforts. College students can pay off school debts, baby boomers can build retirement funds, and parents can enjoy earning unlimited income, working around their family schedules from the comfort of home.

Stable network marketing companies offer free leadership and business training platforms. And since the model is based on people helping people, the more you help, the larger your team grows! You don't take from the earnings of others to receive your commissions, but are rewarded directly for your personal product sales and also those flowing through your organization. Much like a franchise, business centers are duplicated at multiple levels and each person participating in it receives exactly the same tools and opportunity as you do.

People are attracted to leaders who give value and inspire them. Network marketing leaders take advantage of education through popular network marketing books, seminars, and podcasts. They encourage people to reach their goals and begin by meeting people where they are. Leaders understand it's not about them, but it's about serving others and listening to what they want. To be an effective leader in this industry, you must have the best interests of other people at heart.

The business is all about duplication, and creating an organization of positive people will also generate success by their duplicatable actions, attitudes, and work ethic. Network marketing is all about growing and enhancing skills. It also focuses on reaching for and meeting goals—one step at a time.

Network marketing companies usually assign a point value to each product. To qualify for commissions, every business builder must personally purchase a certain number of points worth of product each month. Having your products automatically shipped to you every 30 days is a convenient way to ensure everyone meets their full qualifications. (You can select different products each month). If the autoship involves consumables, an added bonus is you get to eat your overhead! My chosen network marketing emphasis is in the wellness sector, so my autoship helps keep my body and my business healthy and strong!

By the way, health-related products comprise a $4.2 trillion worldwide industry, according to the Global Wellness Institute. So if your network marketing company concentrates in that niche and operates across several countries, your opportunity for business growth is even more substantial.

TIPS ON SELECTING THE RIGHT NETWORK MARKETING COMPANY

Choose a network marketing company meeting your unique lifestyle and needs, since your loyalty will open the gates to financial freedom. Following are five guidelines to assist you on your quest:

(1) *Select a company that markets superb quality consumable products.* To operate a business with the highest income potential, you'll need to market *consumable products.* It's also crucial to find a company where people will buy, use and reorder the products regardless if they make any money or not. It's essential to have REAL customers! You will also need to take and believe in the products yourself.

(2) *Find out how long the company has been in business.* The benchmark of stability is five years since, statistically, most network marketing companies who fail do it within this time frame. Since your goal is to create a long-term residual income, you want to make sure the company will stand the test of time.

(3) *Understand the company's compensation plan.* There are many types of comp plans in the industry. Examine your prospective company's plan to determine if it's easy to understand and explain to others. Is it lucrative and fair, rewarding efforts at all tiers or just top achievers? Each company sets up a defined matrix of levels. I favor the hybrid binary with unlimited depth. In this structure, you enroll two people who each enroll two people and your matrix goes from there. Your two teams (also called "legs") form the example of a matrix that goes narrow and deep.

(4) *Investigate the platforms for company-sponsored training and support.* For greatest success, learn all you can about the network marketing industry. If your company provides tools with which to learn and market your business, you'll want to take advantage of them. This instruction could include both product and business training in the form of videos and podcasts, and live events such as conventions and conferences. The top companies also provide a customizable replicated website where you can access these resources at the click of a mouse.

(5) *Research to see if the principals are ethical leaders in the field.* Look for honest and trustworthy people at the helm. The company should be led by knowledgeable and effective leaders, complemented by a solid scientific research and development department, an energetic marketing team, and other strategic business professionals. The principals should support and encourage the worker

bees (distributors) out in the field and make decisions that will be in their best interest. The company should also be a member of the Direct Selling Association, since the DSA only allows ethical network marketing companies to join their organization.

FINAL THOUGHTS

Jimmy Smith, a network marketing multi-millionaire, shares his recipe for success:

- Find a good company that suits you
- Find a product that suits you
- Become a student of network marketing
- Get laser-focused in your efforts

"Once you understand the mathematics of network marketing, you cannot fail. The hardest thing you have to do is talk to people. This business is so simple, it's scary! For a small investment of a few hundred dollars, you could become a millionaire. When you make a lot of money, financial managers come out of the woodwork. I always tell them, 'Look, I invested $500 in products and 11 years later made $36.7 million from the efforts of myself and my family. If you have a better deal, start talking. If you don't have a better deal, start listening!'"[1]

I still enjoy working as an advertising and marketing copywriter (now with my own freelance business). However, I complement those endeavors by participating in network marketing. If financial freedom is *The One Big Thing* for you, too, you just might consider becoming a network marketing professional. The business model supplies a level playing field to people from all walks of life and offers unlimited income potential. The beauty is that you can help countless others achieve their financial freedom goals, too. Success is within reach of every person who takes network marketing seriously.

---

[1] Eric Worre YouTube video interview. Jimmy Smith Million Dollar Interview Part 3-NMPRO #904. Retrieved from https://youtu.be/dluanOy_sU4 on July 16, 2019

About Debbie

Debbie Neumayer is an accomplished journalist, copywriter, and health book author. Although she enjoys writing about many subjects, she specializes in science, nutrition, and natural medicine. One of her unique talents is the ability to transcribe advanced-level clinical information into language the average consumer will understand and enjoy reading.

For more than two decades, Debbie served as a corporate copywriter for major players in the natural products industry, including Enrich International (now part of Unicity). She has authored many titles for Woodland Publishing through the years, including *Honey: Nature's Sweetest Benefits* and *Magnesium: The Miracle Mineral Most of Us Are Missing*.

Debbie's professional background is also rich in newspaper and online journalism, primarily writing feature articles. She has served as both a freelance and staff reporter covering such diverse topics as Romanian orphan adoptions, air pollution, and saving a cherished ancient structure from demolition. The future of a revered historic building and its impending doom hung in the balance until Debbie teamed up with a concerned group determined to save it from destruction. She wrote a series of local newspaper articles that kept the community informed and engaged with the subject. The building ended up becoming transformed into a beautiful library with reception rooms and more, and today is proudly known as The Provo City Library at Academy Square.

She operates a targeted marketing and communications business where she happily serves customers' writing needs, which includes interviewing subjects for bios, profiles, case studies, press releases, and feature stories. Creating video scripts is also one of her passions. Credits include scripting *Living in a Toxic World* which garnered a Gold Remi Award, two Telly Awards, and a Grand Goldie Award at the 39th WorldFest-Houston International Film Festival (2006). She has also written and directed several amateur one-act plays, including a melodrama which was produced four times.

Debbie enjoys teaching entrepreneurs and takes them from the inception of an idea to completing their enterprise in her book, *Hello Money; Goodbye*

Boss! She also enjoys sharing the benefits of network marketing with people interested in starting franchise-like businesses in the natural health field.

Debbie endeavors to keep her skillset sharp and recently fulfilled the rigid requirements of an expository writing class through Harvard University. She is currently finishing a book manuscript covering the causes, prevention, and natural treatment of cancer—a subject she has researched for more than three decades.

You can connect with Debbie at:

- https://www.debbieneumayer.com/
- https://www.linkedin.com/in/deborahlneumayer/
- https://twitter.com/DebbieNeumayer

CHAPTER 7

FINDING YOUR UNIQUE LEADERSHIP VOICE, ONE DECISION AT A TIME

BY EVELYN CAMPOS DIAZ

MONICA'S PET PIG

"A pig. Really? I can't believe they'd do this to me. Do they think I'm stupid?" Sally, a new leader, slumped down into my guest chair. Monica, Sally's employee, brought her pet pig into the company's kitchen. Monica wanted to give it to her co-worker. She housed it in a box underneath the break table until the end of their shift and then gave it to her co-worker to take home. This happened while Sally was out on leave. As soon as Sally returned, gleeful employees whispered about what happened. Clearly, Sally was taking this personally, first, because it occurred while she was away. Secondly, Sally took policy violations personally.

Sally was an intelligent, talented new leader with good values, so I asked her: what kind of an organization do you want to have? She seemed stunned by the question. Sally had been told to report to HR, tell the story, and get instructions on how to proceed. While I am sure she expected to hear the outrage and be told what "punishment" should issue, I paused to ask her the *real* question so as to give her some *real* help. What kind of an organization do you want to have? I went on to explain: "You can be reactive or take the leap to be proactive. You can shape your workforce into what you *want* them to be." Sally wanted to hear more about the latter.

What any new leader wants are the same things we all want as human beings: trust, to be liked, to be respected, etc. The harsh reality is that the position of leadership alone does not provide these. Often it is easier to shape behavior by imposing discipline as opposed to finding ways to reward positive behavior. Of course, there is little positive behavior to be found in bringing a live pig to work and storing it, of all places, in the food preparation area. What Sally could do, however, was take advantage of the fact that so many employees knew the story. We talked about bringing in Monica and talking to her about the behavior. We also discussed ways that we could use the behavior for a positive result. By asking Monica her thought process and identifying where it went off the rails, we were able to shape her thinking into a better direction. We also took the opportunity to educate her regarding all the health/safety violations. Lastly, we talked about how we could not only correct Monica's behavior but also that of others in the building.

The result was phenomenal. Everyone expected Monica to be punished. When she was not, that changed the perception of employees and other leaders in the building. Monica became a champion of health/safety protocols. We were about Sally and the organization's mission: having a safe and productive workplace. By shaping the existing workforce rather than knee-jerking to the discipline stick, we were able to use Sally's natural leadership to bring about a real change in her department. The other benefit was that Sally earned the respect and trust she was after, not by "showing them who's boss," but by showing them whom she trusted them to become.

JONATHAN'S BREAKTHROUGH

Jonathan arrived 15 minutes early to the conference room. He supervised many personnel who inspected railroad tracks for a metropolitan subway system. This work, done when the system was closed, involved a visual inspection of each inch of track to detect defects before they became a problem. Jason, his employee, arrived a bit later than the scheduled meeting time, looking disheveled and rushed. Jonathan said to Jason: "Why are you late? You are always late!" Then he turned to me and said: "This is the problem that I have." I put up my hand and said: "Hold on a minute, let's start from the beginning."

I was there to mediate between two good employees who each harbored adverse perceptions of the other. Jonathan, the supervisor, felt Jason had an "attitude." Jason felt Jonathan was a "bear" of a supervisor. A breakthrough moment came in the middle of the session. Jonathan said that he learned from his "sponsor" how to keep himself on task and on time and that he wished that Jason would learn the same lesson. Jason's eyes lit up and he said, "Sponsor? Are you in AA? I did not know that. So am I!" Jonathan uncrossed his arms, sat up in his chair and leaned forward to talk *with* Jason. Sensing the sea change, I asked to leave the room as each was now finally talking with the other. About one hour later, Jonathan opened the door and I saw the two men shaking each other's hands. As they parted, Jonathan said: "See you later, right?" Jason responded: "Yes, and *on time!*" They both laughed and went on their way.

While this is not a typical revelation at the workplace, it is a great example of what can happen when leaders get caught up in their own feedback loops. Jonathan was an experienced, successful leader but he had become mired (as many leaders do) in the minutiae of managing a represented workforce. He was focusing all of his attention on the next report, the next job, the next "tardy" by an employee. He lost sight of the need for a leader to see the mission of the organization as the goal, not the busywork in front of him.

Every worker is a human being with a set of circumstances that drive their everyday lives. Sometimes leaders forget to address the human beings that work for them and we miss the opportunity to forge a bond that can inspire beyond the day-to-day work tasks. The company's mission is to provide safe, reliable transportation for the metropolitan area. Jason has a critically important role to play in that mission. Jason cannot help but have his work life carry over into his personal life, and vice-versa. By breaking through and seeing Jason as a whole person, Jonathan was able to redirect the purpose in the meeting towards finding a way to get a good worker to be better, and thus fulfilling the organization's mission. This is not always easy, but it is essential for business survival. All leaders must look for, find, and act on their authentic selves: connect with their employees to drive excellence in the workplace.

BRIAN'S SPECTRUM OF CHOICES

A few years ago, I was told a very interesting story about an Air Force officer, Brian, who faced a difficult dilemma when he was told by his legal department that he had to discharge one of his airmen, Mitch. Mitch had filed a false claim for reimbursement to himself, a serious infraction for which the legal department advised Brian to initiate a discharge action. Brian was torn, as he felt that this was too strong a way in which to deal with a first offense.

Brian received a call from the defense counsel assigned to handle Mitch's defense. Brian indicated it seemed like a done deal, until the defense counsel asked what seemed an unusual question: is this really the way you want to handle this as a leader? Brian thought about it, and then said he was unaware he had any options. The defense counsel explained that under the military code of justice, Brian was being advised by the legal department to take a course of corrective action, but that ultimately it was up to Brian to impose discipline in the manner he felt was the most appropriate to maintain "good order and discipline" in his squadron. The defense counsel then asked Brian to "tell me about your servicemember." Brian eagerly launched into having served with him overseas, they had been through "thick and thin" together, that he saw the grit of that airman and that he felt it was "unfair" to discharge him because Brian knew that Mitch did not mean to commit a crime when he made the false claim. Ultimately, Brian decided to impose a lesser action on Mitch which allowed Mitch to continue to serve.

Brian was relying on his "experts" to the point that he forgot his role and responsibility as a leader. The result was that he was ready to do that which he felt was detrimental to his workforce because he was advised a certain way. Leaders are put in their roles for a reason. They have the authority, and the responsibility, to make the decisions necessary to bring about the best for their subordinates and ultimately fulfill the organization's mission. When leaders hide behind so-called experts (i.e., HR, legal, etc.) to avoid making difficult decisions, they are not being true to themselves and not fulfilling the reasons for which they were made leaders in the first place. To be clear, HR and legal serve very important roles in any organization and leaders should always give weight to their advice. (Hopefully these experts are guiding you transparently to examine and weigh your thoughts, much like in the examples of Sally and Jonathan above.) Ultimately, however, we have to remember that what the experts are doing is providing *advice*. They provide options along a spectrum of risk from which leaders can make the ultimate decision based upon what leaders believe to be the best option for their organizations. Sometimes it can be difficult to stay authentic to the leader voice inside you, but you need to trust the instincts and abilities that enabled you to achieve the leadership role in the first place.

YOUR UNIQUE LEADERSHIP VOICE

Leaders expect that they will bring others along with them on a journey toward a shared common goal. This journey balances, tenuously, inspiration to and support for those you lead. What may seem to you as an endless series of routine decisions will, in fact, be used by your employees to determine if they have trust in you and the organization. This trust is essential for them so that they can therefore give their very best to the company's mission. Your employees will be watching closely not only to see if you have compassion, but also to see if you can act on it. This is especially noticeable when leaders find the courage to do the right thing and discipline an employee who deserves it as a way, and in a way, that supports those who are doing the right thing. For every decision you make, there will be those who support and criticize in equal measure. The key is not to take routine decisions for granted. With laser focus, return to the touchstone of your leadership every time: what is the best thing for your organization, consistent with your vision of its future.

These three leaders were at pivotal points in who they were as leaders. How did they get there? One decision, or non-decision, at a time. Today's business environment requires us to make multiple decisions at a rapid pace:

- who will work overtime?
- who gets to lead the project?
- who gets vacation time and in what order?
- who will write the synopsis?
- who will get the complex job?
- ...etc.

We could get trapped into losing sight of our unique leadership voice as well as the company's mission when making these routine decisions. These can sneak up on unsuspecting leaders resulting in the wrong conclusions about who they are as leaders. Therefore, align all your leadership decisions with your unique leadership voice. My "One Big Thing" is this: stay true to your voice, your unique leadership voice, and apply it to every decision, large or small, that you make along your journey to success.

About Evelyn

Evelyn Campos Diaz has had the good fortune of experiencing inspirational leaders throughout her formative years. This may explain her passion with leadership development that inevitably led her to become one of the preeminent Human Resources Executives in the healthcare industry. She has served in many roles in Human Resources for the last twenty years, but feels that it pales in comparison to the joy she had found as a wife and mother.

Evelyn holds a Juris Doctor degree and an MBA degree with a concentration in Organizational Leadership along with a number of specialty certifications in her field, including being a certified MBTI® practitioner. Her accomplishments include winning the 2014 HRLA Leadership Award of Greater Washington, DC and various speaking engagements including at SHRM's annual conference in 2015.

Evelyn has extensive experience strategizing, designing and developing effective leadership development programs for executives and leaders, but can also be found painting, hiking and being a sci-fi geek. She welcomes connections via her LinkedIn profile, especially from that next generation of Human Resources leaders.

CHAPTER 8

DICTION AND TONE SET THE TONE FOR YOUR BUSINESS

BY JAMIE ZISKA,
Executive Business Coach

"Work life balance." "Great work culture." These are catch phrases that companies are using as bait to attract top talent for their organizations. No matter the current fad phrase, there are some key things to keep in mind in order to attract and retain quality employees. People often seem to choose the wrong diction and tone especially in business. The words that we choose can inadvertently impact our work culture and how the employees (and eventually their customers) perceive the company.

Therefore, it is critical to understand how diction and tone impact your business and your ability to hire and retain the highest quality professionals. How we talk to our employees eventually appears in how we talk to our customers too. No one wants to be talked down to, nor do they want people talking to them in harsh tones. It is important to see how our words impact those around us. We have all had a supervisor come over and ask, "why did you do that," and suddenly we are thrust into defending ourselves and our work. That doesn't set the right tone for productivity and longevity. Whenever possible, when you are questioning "why" something was done, try to question the process and not the person.

I'd like to start with a story about Ana. Ana was a manager at a manufacturing facility. She had several employees under her supervision, and part of the group's job was calculating final weights for shipping out product. These calculations were manual – meaning that a handwritten weight sheet was brought to the group to add up (sometimes several pages long, each page having up to 100 numbers). After doing the math, the group had to create a bill of lading and an invoice. For a simple load, the process took about 20 minutes. With more complex loads, the process would take an hour. One day, Stanley comes barging into Ana's office infuriated and says, "Why is your team taking so long to do these bills of lading? It's never taken this long before."

Stanley knew the basics of the process but made an assumption that he knew where the bottleneck was. He knew that Ana's team relied on paperwork being delivered to them from the plant. What Stanley did not know was that when truckers called in asking when loads would be done, the person answering the phone would ask Mark, the plant manager, when it would be done. Mark would tell them the production end time and not add any additional time to production time for paperwork processing. The drivers would arrive at the time designated by Mark. The product was made but the order was not ready to ship because the office had not had time to process the paperwork. What seemed like it was taking the "office" a long time to process, was really a misconstrued time being conveyed to the drivers.

This story illustrates how it is important to know more than the issue at hand – but to ask questions about the process instead of assuming you know it. There may be more to the process than what you realize, and without asking questions and instead making accusations, you are positioning yourself to be the "bad guy". So, you may be asking yourself, "How could Stanley have asked a similar question without putting Ana and her team into defense mode?"

Again, question the process not the people. When you discuss the process instead of the people doing it, it is less personal. Stanley could have asked a series of questions such as, "Ana, what is our current process for getting drivers out of the office? What part of the process does your team handle? What is your biggest struggle in getting the paperwork finished before the driver arrives?" There are questions that could also help involve Ana in resolving the perceived issue that could be asked, including: If you could fix anything in this process what would you change? How would that change benefit your team and/or the organization?

By asking questions that are about the process, one is no longer attacking the person but instead looking for a cooperative effort to improve a given situation. Questioning is amazing, but keep in mind that you need to be an active listener as well. When the person is responding, do not formulate your response right away. Really listen to what you are being told. Your first response after a series of questions should be to recap what you heard. Only after you confirm that you have heard the situation clearly should you respond. Again, keep your response about the process and not the person.

This conscientious examining of our diction and tone can extend beyond the simple 'how we do things' into 'who we value or don't value'. Asking questions about the process removes the personal feelings from the conversation. Actively listening shows you are really interested in resolving the issues instead of attacking the person. Everyone wants and needs to feel heard.

How you speak to people and about people shows how you think of them. Let me tell you about Julie and Clark. Clark was a head sales person, and Julie was in charge of processing key bids and contracts that were crucial for Clark to do his job. There was a large contract underway and Clark had made several large changes to the pricing along the way. Julie had stayed late several nights in a row to make sure that all of the other contracts were delivered on time. This particular evening, Clark came over an hour past when Julie was supposed to leave, requesting some major changes. "Clark, these changes will take at least two hours to complete. How about we finish them early tomorrow morning and send to the client after you review them?"

"I don't care what you need to do, get these done tonight," Clark demanded from Julie.

"When are you going to be reviewing these?" Julie replied, trying to remain calm.

"I'll review them first thing in the morning. Send them to me tonight." Clark barked.

Clark knew that he would not be reviewing the documents, and he knew that it was after 6 pm and that Julie started by 7 am. When confronted with the option of sending them the next day, all that he could focus on was that he wanted Julie to do it now. It didn't matter what heroic efforts it would take from her. It didn't matter that she had plans for after work that evening that she would have to cancel.

How would this make a person feel? What reactions would you have in a similar situation? Now translate this to your business. Are you asking for anyone to make heroic efforts to get something done, when you do not have any intention of reviewing it soon? Or are you giving adequate time, available to answer questions and reviewing items in a spirit of cooperation. Ultimately your team needs to be focused on the same end result that you are.

The diction and tone you utilize most is the message that you are sending to your employees, but quite likely to your clients too. What is the message that you want to send? Do you want to send that you are unapproachable and demanding? Or do you want to set the tone of an open door policy that actually means something to your employees? Do you actively listen – or are you busy formulating your reaction instead of hearing them all the way through?

Your words have meaning. Let that sink in for a moment. *Your words have meaning.* Whether they are written or spoken, your words have meaning. Your words will impact others – for good or bad. Your words will motivate or destroy. If you are tempted to speak or write words that may hurt, take a deep breath and imagine how you would react to someone speaking those words to you. Once you have evaluated your words, then take action. Speak words that will convey your message, but also, whenever possible, choose words that uplift and empower others. By doing so, you will lead them to be more invested in you, your organization and putting forth their best efforts. Your culture is set by the words you and your team use. This culture not only impacts your internal clients (employees) but it will bleed out into the world of your customers.

People are often hiding behind the computer screen these days. They can easily send messages that are hurtful and hateful, demeaning or accusatory because they are not having to face the person face-to-face or over the phone. It is easy to forget that behind that computer screen, on the other side is another human being. They deserve and crave the same respect and desire to move the organization forward.

People choose to follow leaders because they understand where the leader is going, what the message is and more importantly, they relate to the leader. People relate to their leaders because of the messages their leaders send with their diction and tone. What message are you sending and how does that differ from the message that you want to be sending? What message do you want to have your employees send to your clients? Are you customer-focused? Or are you a tyrant? These will be evident to not only your employees, but also your clients.

THE ONE BIG THING

Your clients will eventually understand your culture based on how they are treated. The question becomes, what can you do about this? How can you know if you are speaking empowering, encouraging words versus inadvertently destructive words? This can be the hardest step of all, but you must learn to listen. Listen without judgement. Listen without consequences. Ask open-ended questions and wait for responses. People will start talking. You cannot judge during this time, do not think about your response or get defensive when you are asking your employees for feedback. Listen and repeat what your employee is saying in your own words. This will allow people to feel heard and understood.

Let's break this down into easy-to-follow steps, shall we?

1) Speak with clarity and use empowering words.
2) Listen to others as if what they are saying is important and valued.
3) Do not judge when others are speaking (especially employees).
4) Repeat back what they said to confirm clarity and validate the person.
5) Ask open questions to encourage collaboration.
6) Question processes and not people's actions whenever possible.
7) Pause before speaking or writing hurtful words. Once released you cannot take them back.

People want to follow a leader. To lead effectively you must not only speak empowering words, but also know when to listen and really hear the issues. Listening and speaking with the right tone and diction will help your culture be one that people want to be a part of. If you aren't sure where to start, there are a lot of great articles online, a variety of coaches and books dedicated to speaking empowering words.

Build the business you desire by speaking words that will help propel your business forward.

About Jamie

Jamie Ziska, better known as JZ, is the head coach and founder of Retaining Excellence LLC. JZ has a passion for teaching others to be cognizant about their diction, tone, and the understanding that their words impact others' lives. She works with executives, managers and business owners to learn to listen and create a work culture that top talent will not only be attracted to, but will want to be a part of.

JZ has a passion for working with other people to recognize how diction, tone, and non-verbal cues can impact people throughout organizations – from employees to customers. In this time of electronic communications, it is easy to forget that on the other side of the communication is a person – a living, breathing human being that has emotions and feelings. JZ loves bringing the people back into the light and refocusing on what matters.

While JZ has a bachelor's degree, she is a constant learner. She has additional certifications in life coaching, health coaching, belief clearing and business coaching.

To reach JZ you can contact her at:

- www.linkedin.com/in/jziskaretainingexcellence

CHAPTER 9

TRANSFORMING YOUR BUSINESS INTO A BLOCKBUSTER

BY NICK NANTON AND JW DICKS

> *The biggest thing is to let your voice be heard, let your story be heard.*
> ~ Dwyane Wade

When you tell your story in the right way, you can achieve a level of success that's almost criminal.

Take Jordan Belfort for example. This super-salesman made $20,000 by hawking Italian Ice from Styrofoam coolers in summers down at the beach when he was in college – but his ambition was to be a dentist. However, he quit the Baltimore College of Tooth Surgery on his first day, after the dean told the new class that if they wanted to make a lot of money, they were in the wrong place.

Instead, Belfort became a notorious stock swindler who made millions bilking small investors – and at one point employed 1,000 people to help him do it. The Feds finally ended up catching up with all his scams, and he ended up being sentenced to 22 months in jail. The government also sold off all his assets to pay back the victims.

End of story? No, actually just the beginning.

While in prison, Belfort met Tommy Chong, one-half of the hugely popular comedy duo Cheech and Chong. Chong was in jail for helping promote a business that sold drug paraphernalia over the Internet. When Belfort told Chong about all his insane adventures running his stockswindling company, Chong advised him to write a book about them. That advice turned to be a critical turning point.

The finished book, *The Wolf of Wall Street*, became a huge bestseller. And you're also probably aware that it was made into a lavishly-produced movie hit directed by Hollywood legend, Martin Scorsese, with Leonardo DiCaprio playing the part of Belfort. The critically-acclaimed film was nominated for 5 Oscars.

More importantly for Belfort, the celebrity status he gained from having his story told through the book and movie fueled a business comeback as a motivational speaker. That's because, even though the book and film clearly showed his criminal activity, it also clearly showed his skill at sales, a skill many are willing to pay large sums of money to acquire.

And that's why Belfort now earns tens of thousands of dollars for each speech and seminar that he's hired to do – although he calls what he teaches: the art of "*ethically* persuading." And we certainly hope he's sticking to that "ethically" part.

STORIES: THE FOUNDATION OF SUCCESS

Belfort's experience illustrates the power of stories, which has been heavily researched and validated (and is discussed at length in our *StorySelling*™ book). To summarize a couple of important points here, studies show that our brains *love* stories because they help us make sense of the world. Stories actually hit the pleasure centers of our minds – which causes us to often disregard the facts if they get in the way of a narrative we want to believe. Finally, we actually *need* stories – without them, we might not be able to make sense of our lives and how to approach them. We have a basic need to connect the dots of our existence, and the way we do that is through *stories*.

That's why, as Belfort discovered, telling the right story in the right way in the right medium can take you to a level of business success you might ordinarily think is out of reach. That's the principle we've built our own business on – and we've practiced what we preach.

When we first opened the doors of our Celebrity Branding Agency®, one of the first things we knew we needed to do was write a book to explain who we were and what we did. That book became our very first bestseller, *Celebrity Branding You*™ – but it wasn't written for the purpose of being successful; it was written for the purpose of explaining what our Celebrity Branding techniques were all about and why they *worked*.

Result? That book got us a lot of business and really sent us on our way.

Back in 2012, we realized it was time to write another book that would amplify the importance of exactly what we're talking about in this chapter – telling your story in the most impactful way through movies, books and other media. That book, *StorySelling*™, happily became an even bigger success, rising to #4 on *The Wall Street Journal*'s non-fiction list and to the #1 paid non-fiction book on the Amazon Kindle.

Result? More people understood what we did at a deeper level – and were ready to do business with us.

So – why a book? Couldn't we explain these things to potential clients in person? Or over the phone?

Well, yes, we could – but we still wouldn't be able to cover the hundreds of pages of content in our books. You can only communicate so much in a conversation before you get tired of talking – or the person on the other side gets tired of listening to you!

But there was another bigger reason to present our ideas this way. Because our information was in a best-selling book, it ended up having much more weight and credibility than if it was just conveyed in a sales pitch.

In a way, putting your message out through a book is really a big test: You have to really have something to say in order to pull one off, you just can't fake your way through one. And anyone who read our latest book would discover a mountain of verifiable facts, proven strategies and high-profile case studies that support what our agency offered our clients.

What it comes down to is this: What you do for your customers and clients involves *your* area of expertise, not theirs. And they may not necessarily understand what makes your specific professional process both different and more effective than your competitors' – and why it will ultimately benefit them greatly to hire you or your company.

A book is a managed, prestigious way to help them understand: It allows you to tell *your* story and present your unique selling proposition in a clear and powerful way. When done correctly, you not only explain the key to *your* success – you also explain why it could be the key to *their* success, in terms of what the product or service you're selling can do for them.

But, as Jordan Belfort found out for himself, a book serves only as the foundation of your StorySelling™. To really attain a whole new level of success? You must build your business into a blockbuster.

GOING BEYOND BEING JUST ANOTHER BUSINESS

Here are a few book titles we're sure many of you have heard of (if not read):

- *The One Minute Manager*
- *Who Moved My Cheese?*
- *The Seven Habits of Highly Effective People*
- *Eat that Frog!*

The above were, of course, all highly influential business books that crystalized their authors' philosophies in an easy-to-grasp concept (and, by the way, the last one happened to be co-authored by Brian Tracy, the legend whose name you'll find on this book).

Now, because of the phenomenal success of these books, because of the way they resonated with their readers, the authors were able to build their personal consulting businesses into *blockbusters*.

But they didn't reach blockbuster status by simply publishing one book. No, they did it through media appearances, videos, in-person appearances and seminars, online marketing, and magazine and newspaper interviews. They continued the story laid out in their books into other media, just as Jordan Belfort continued his into a hit movie; they reinforced their essential narratives over and over and over until they owned a substantial segment of their audiences.

This, of course, is nothing new. Walt Disney started his incredible entertainment empire by producing a short black-and-white cartoon featuring a talking mouse. He continued to expand his core brand story, first into animated features like *Snow White and the Seven Dwarfs*, then into live-action movies like *Mary Poppins*, and finally into theme park game-changers like Disneyland.

But what if Uncle Walt had just continued to make cartoon shorts? Would he have ever been able to build the awesome multi-billion-

THE ONE BIG THING

dollar blockbuster business that still dominates the Hollywood arena today? Of course not.

Then consider Donald Trump, who not only has written many best-sellers, but has also had his own game show (*Trump Card*), reality show (*The Apprentice*) and has even hosted WrestleMania events! But even with all his different ventures, both in entertainment and business, he always preserves his basic story and persona – and carries it through in everything he does. You don't confuse Donald Trump with anybody else, ever!

Building on your story and finding new and different ways to tell it is what truly transforms your business from a successful one into a *legendary* one. When you continue to deliver the same narrative across a broad range of venues and media, people remember that narrative – and you. You become your own version of Starbucks, McDonald's or any other world-famous brand – and you become an instantly-recognized authority in your field, as well as the go-to person for your specialty.

What are the advantages of that? Well, there are at least three very big ones:

- **You can charge more money for what you do.**
  When you enter the rarified atmosphere of a business blockbuster, you achieve a name and reputation that people are willing to pay top dollar for in order to gain access. Moguls like Donald Trump and Richard Branson make millions just lending their names to other people's business ventures, just because everyone knows who they are and what they represent – and because it delivers a level of prestige that's unmistakable.
- **You will wield more influence.**
  When you achieve blockbuster status, people and organizations are more willing to listen to what you have to say, even if they've never done business with you. The right word from you can have an enormous impact on others' dealings, which gives you more personal power out in the marketplace.

- **You can dominate your field.**
Apple is an obvious example of a blockbuster business. They've always had a consistent and dynamic sense of StorySelling that's created not just customers, but disciples! The pay-off for that long-term vision has been a company that not only completely dominates their particular slice of the computer market, but also music distribution through their iTunes platform, as well as the cellphone industry through their phenomenally popular iPhone. Because they told such an incredible brand story, consumers were willing to follow them into whatever field they decided to diversity into.

THE BUILDING BLOCKS OF A BLOCKBUSTER

As you can see, being a blockbuster business delivers some awesome rewards. So – are you ready to kick your business up to blockbuster status? Here are a few pointers from us on how to do just that:

Building Block #1: Drill Down on Your Story
Before you start StorySelling, make sure you've got a narrative that will not only attract the kind of clients you want to attract, but also accurately reflects who you are and what you do. Making sure you have the right story in place *before* you aggressively StorySell is THE most important step you have to take. If you're pretending to be something you're not, it will catch up to you; that's why, before you put a lot of time, effort and money into your StorySelling, you should make sure your story isn't going to blow up in your face down the line.

We can return to Jordan Belfort for a good example of that. As we noted, he's now selling himself as an ethical persuader – unfortunately, he's recently been accused of hiding the money he's making down under in Australia, so he doesn't have to pay back the people he originally swindled! If that's true, his new StorySelling attempts already have an unhappy ending.

Building Block #2: Be a Person
It's okay to show some of your warts in your StorySelling – as a matter of fact, it's preferable. The more you can show you're a human being, flaws and all, the more relatable and the more memorable you are. Obviously, don't take this to extremes, although it does work out for some people!

Building Block #3: Be Unconventional
We quickly passed over an interesting item a little earlier in this chapter, so we're going to repeat it here – *Donald Trump hosted WrestleMania events*! Now, that might be the last place you'd expect to see The Donald, sandwiched between two mammoth wrestlers getting ready to break chairs over each other's heads – but the fact is, it does him some substantial good, from a StorySelling perspective. Think about it – his appearances at these matches (a) get Trump more attention, (b) expand his exposure to a whole different audience, and (c) actually kind of fits in with his aggressive brand!

The unconventional gets attention – and the more you do things that your competitors don't do, the more you stand out. As long as it fits in with your narrative and you're not doing something that will land you in jail, embrace the weird – and even post about it on Facebook and Twitter!

Building Block #4: Don't Be Camera-Shy
If you're like many people, you probably don't like to look in the mirror more than you have to – but, unless your brand story is that you're a recluse like Howard Hughes was, you're going to have to get over the impulse to hide whenever anyone snaps a photo with their iPhone. A vital part of StorySelling involves showing yourself as much as possible – in films, online videos, the above-mentioned social media platforms, even on the cover of your book, so again, people can bond with you on a human level. The more potential clients feel like they know you, the more they will trust you and the more willing they will be to do business with you.

Building Block #5: Keep Your Core Value Front and Center
Most blockbuster brand stories can be boiled down to a couple of words that really define what they're all about. Apple? Innovation. Disney? Family entertainment. Wal-Mart? Low prices.

The word or words you use to define what you and your business are all about represent your *core value*, the thing that, when all is said and done, represents you the best. This quality should be present in *everything* you do from a StorySelling standpoint – because it's what you want people to take away more than anything else.

The great thing about creating a blockbuster business brand is that, once in place, it continues to generate its own success; people recognize it and reward it, often just because it *is* a known quantity. Of course, not every business can achieve blockbuster status – that's why those who do are perceived as being incredibly special and unique.

You too can StorySell yourself to greatness if you take the steps to tell your tale in as many different high-profile media as possible. You may not become *The Wolf of Wall Street* – but you could become the Mogul of Main Street!

About JW

JW Dicks, Esq., is the CEO of DN Agency, an Inc. 5000 Multimedia Company that represents over 3000 clients in 63 countries.

He is a *Wall Street Journal* Best-Selling Author® who has authored or co-authored over 47 books, a 5-time Emmy® Award-winning Executive Producer and a Broadway Show Producer.

JW is an XPrize Innovation Board member, Chairman of the Board of the National Retirement Council™, Chairman of the Board of the National Academy of Best-Selling Authors®, Board Member of the National Association of Experts, Writers and Speakers®, and a Board Member of the International Academy of Film Makers®.

He has been quoted on business and financial topics in national media such as *USA Today, The Wall Street Journal, Newsweek, Forbes, CNBC.com*, and *Fortune Magazine Small Business*.

JW has co-authored books with legends like Jack Canfield, Brian Tracy, Tom Hopkins, Dr. Nido Qubein, Steve Forbes, Richard Branson, Michael Gerber, Dr. Ivan Misner, and Dan Kennedy.

JW has appeared and interviewed on business television shows airing on ABC, NBC, CBS, and FOX affiliates around the country and co-produces and syndicates a line of franchised business television shows such as *Success Today, Wall Street Today, Hollywood Live*, and *Profiles of Success*.

JW and his wife of 47 years, Linda, have two daughters, and four granddaughters. He is a sixth-generation Floridian and splits his time between his home in Orlando and his beach house on Florida's west coast.

About Nick

An Emmy Award-Winning Director and Producer, Nick Nanton, Esq., produces media and branded content for top thought leaders and media personalities around the world. Recognized as a leading expert on branding and storytelling, Nick has authored more than two dozen Best-Selling books (including *The Wall Street Journal* Best-Seller *StorySelling*™) and produced and directed more than 50 documentaries, earning 11 Emmy Awards and 26 nominations. Nick speaks to audiences internationally on the topics of branding, entertainment, media, business and storytelling at major universities and events.

As the CEO of DNA Media, Nick oversees a portfolio of companies including: The Dicks + Nanton Agency (an international agency with more than 3000 clients in 63 countries), Dicks + Nanton Productions, Ambitious.com and DNA Films. Nick is an award-winning director, producer and songwriter who has worked on everything from large scale events to television shows with the likes of Steve Forbes, Ivanka Trump, Sir Richard Branson, Larry King, Jack Nicklaus, Rudy Ruettiger (inspiration for the Hollywood Blockbuster, *RUDY*), Brian Tracy, Jack Canfield (*The Secret*, creator of the *Chicken Soup for the Soul* Series), and many more.

Nick has been seen in *USA Today*, *The Wall Street Journal*, *Newsweek*, *BusinessWeek*, *Inc. Magazine*, *The New York Times*, *Entrepreneur® Magazine*, *Forbes* and *Fast Company*, and has appeared on ABC, NBC, CBS, and FOX television affiliates across the country, as well as on CNN, FOX News, CNBC, and MSNBC coast-to-coast.

Nick is a member of the Florida Bar, a member of The National Academy of Television Arts & Sciences (Home to the EMMYs), co-founder of The National Academy of Best-Selling Authors®, and serves on the Innovation Board of the XPRIZE Foundation, a non-profit organization dedicated to bringing about "radical breakthroughs for the benefit of humanity" through incentivized competition and best known for its Ansari XPRIZE—which incentivized the first private space flight and was the catalyst for Richard Branson's Virgin Galactic.

Nick also enjoys serving as an Elder at Orangewood Church, working with Young Life, Entrepreneurs International and rooting for the Florida Gators with his wife Kristina and their three children, Brock, Bowen and Addison.

Learn more at:

- www.NickNanton.com
- www.CelebrityBrandingAgency.com

CHAPTER 10

DIVORCE OR DESTINY
TRANSFORM YOUR LIFE BY PRESSING THE RESET BUTTON

BY GEORGE LEE, ESQ.

Watch your thoughts, they become your words;
Watch your words, they become your deeds;
Watch your deeds, they become your habits;
Watch your habits, they become your character;
Watch your character, it becomes your destiny.
~ Lao Tzu

There is an old fable about a donkey that fell into a pit. The animal cried out for hours while its owner tried to figure out what to do. Finally, the owner decided that since the animal was old, and the pit needed to be covered up anyway, he would bury the old donkey right there. He got a shovel and started filling in the pit while the donkey made furious noises, then fell silent. To his surprise, he observed his old donkey jumping out of the pit. How was this possible?

At first, the donkey had cried out of fear. But then the wise animal hit on a plan: as the dirt hit its back, the donkey would shake it off. A mound of earth grew beneath the donkey. Eventually, the mound grew high enough for the donkey to jump out of the pit.

Life is change. As we grow and develop, we may experience ups and downs that we do not always prepare for. Divorce, for instance, is a turning point to press the reset button. For many, pain is optional, but change is inevitable for all.

As an experienced divorce attorney, I have witnessed many painful "battles of roses" that happen in court. During my two decades in and out of the courtroom, it is clear that marital troubles are only the proverbial tip of the iceberg. Those who are going through a divorce are almost always struggling with other life issues. This realization marked a milestone in my career.

Subsequently, I have extended my study to many branches of training: from life-coach training to hypnosis, from NLP (neuro-linguistic programming) technology to modes of transformation methodologies, and from studying spirituality to exploring psychology. In the search for answers to my deepest questions, I created a powerful framework which I call S.W.I.F.T. Transformation coaching to help people tackle life's challenges and achieve transformation.

In one example, Jennifer had insomnia after separation. She lost her sense of direction and felt overburdened by stress. In practicing S.W.I.F.T. visualization techniques, she imagined herself hearing her lawyer congratulating her again and again that her court matter was settled in her favor; soon afterwards, her imagination became a reality! For Jennifer, using this technique helped transform her life.

WHAT IS S.W.I.F.T. TRANSFORMATION™?

S.W.I.F.T. Transformation™ is the integration of five modalities, including the **S**enses, the spoken **W**ord, your **I**magination, **F**aith and **T**hought. It contains five easy steps that anyone can grasp. In coaching clients, we work toward achieving specific goals or wishes by practicing these steps on a daily basis.

To achieve a specific goal, you must first step into to the zone, asking yourself, "How would I feel if my goal is accomplished now?" Imagine all the emotions that would accompany a wish fulfilled. You must truly possess these feelings!

Surely, you've heard of the "placebo effect," or the expression, "fake it 'til you make it." The reason beyond this is fascinating: our minds do not distinguish between internal feelings and outward experience through external sense-perception. As a result, we can fool our minds by assuming an internal feeling through our imagination—our mind will treat such feelings as true and as part of our reality.

How might we apply these learnings to positive intentions charting our own destinies? By integrating the five modalities, we can make transformation possible.

Try this yourself: Think of a goal you wish for. Then, use your imagination to bring the future into the present moment. This will feel real as you evoke each of the five senses: see it in your mind's eye and feel it in your body! Go through some or all of the following practices:

- Imagine yourself seeing the scene of the future when your goal is accomplished
- Imagine yourself feeling that emotion of accomplishment
- Imagine yourself hearing people congratulating you on your achievement
- Imagine yourself touching the future reality with your own hands
- Imagine yourself acting as if your goal has already been accomplished

Before going to bed, or upon arising in the morning, repeat the above exercise. The secret lies in the fact that you have to believe it is possible!

QUENCHING THIRST BY VISUALIZING PLUMS

*Whatever the mind can conceive and believe,
the mind can achieve.*
~ Napoleon Hill

One Chinese legend talks about a famous incident where General Cao spoke of plums as association in order to motivate thirsty soldiers to fight a battle. As the soldiers were exhausted and thirsty under the scorching sun, the general announced that he had discovered a forest of plum trees ahead of the soldiers. Upon hearing "plums," their thirsts were quenched.

There are several psychological truths alluded to in this legend. Our spoken words can create the power of association that brings our sense experience, either from the past or future, to the present. In other words, you can physically experience future emotions in the present moment.

FAITH AS FOUNDATION: JACOB'S STOLEN BLESSING

*When we are no longer able to change a situation,
we are challenged to change ourselves.*
~ Viktor Frankl

In *The Power of Your Subconscious Mind*, Dr. Joseph Murphy aptly said, "The faith that is described in the Bible is a way of thinking, an attitude of mind, an inner certitude, knowing that the idea you fully accept in your conscious mind will be embodied in your subconscious mind and made manifest. Faith is, in a sense, accepting as true what your reason and sense deny." Belief is a critical part of the S.W.I.F.T. Transformation.

The Bible presents numerous allegories that imply the need to liberate our human perceptions from bondage of natural sense-perception to develop a spiritual understanding of truth.

Jacob's story, for instance, is such an allegory that is most misunderstood. For ages, Jacob was called a "deceiver" who stole Esau's blessing. However, the mystery hidden behind the story is: In order to receive blessings, humans need to assume a feeling of wishes fulfilled to supplant the reality. In other words, before achieving your dreams, you need to assume the feeling as if they are fulfilled. Your feeling and wishes must become one!

As the famous American mystic Neville Goddard said, "Feeling is the secret of creation." To realize our dreams or goals, we need first to "assume the feeling of the wish fulfilled and simply ignore everything that denies it." Neville called it the Law of Assumption.

Faith is a positive and powerful mental state where you bypass your conscious mind and see and feel wishes come true in the subconscious before manifestation.

WORDS AS KEYS TO THE POWER OF SELF-FULFILLING PROPHECIES

Life isn't about finding yourself. Life is about creating yourself.
~ George Bernard Shaw

Another part of the S.W.I.F.T. Transformation is how we create the power to fulfill our destinies by calling our dreams into existence. Scientific evidence shows that repetition of certain words with emotions becomes the most powerful energy that can change your reality.

Words are seeds of ideas or thoughts, and once sunk into our subconsciousness, they will manifest in physical forms. How might you unlock the doors to your own destinies simply by declaring the word?

A great example comes from the early 1800's. A French doctor, Émile Coué, transformed the lives of millions of people by the discovery of the placebo effect known as the power of autosuggestion. Dr. Coué devised chanting treatments to treat all diseases, asking his patients to repeat this chant: "Day by day, in every way, I am better and better." History reports countless numbers of success stories – patients cured from of all kinds of diseases – just by the power of words and self-fulfilling prophecies.

In our daily life, our spoken words contain all sorts of suggestions. However, not all suggestions have power over us. For us to be influenced by suggestion, there are three conditions to be fulfilled:

1). Repetition
2). Believing the desired condition as true and complete
3). Accepting the suggestion with emotion

Proverbially, we must "speak to the mountain" and in doing so, we can remove the mountain!

IMAGINATION: THE POWER TO CREATE THE FUTURE

For there is nothing either good or bad, but thinking makes it so.
~ William Shakespeare

In the Bible, human imagination is symbolized by "the fowl of heaven." In Genesis 28, Jacob's dream can be interpreted as a metaphor for human imagination which connects Heaven and earth. Upon his awakening, Jacob was awestruck about his newfound insight of what humans can access through the subconscious. With our faculty of imagination, we have the opportunity to see and create our future.

Scientific research shows that our brain does not distinguish between what is real and what is imaginary – if we imagine a goal, our brain has the ability to treat it as reality. According to Dr. Andrew Newberg, the first step begins with a creative imagination. If you cannot nurture a fantasy about your specific goals, you will not be able to succeed. In other words, our future is first created as reality in our imagination. Anything is possible! Calm down, close your eyes and mentally visualize your wish as fulfilled – seeing it, hearing it, and feeling it.

Recent scientific evidence also shows that "certainty" is only a feeling and a result of unconscious forces at work in the brain. In *The Future of the Body,* Michael Murphy described an interesting experiment conducted by scientists on pregnant women suffering from upset stomachs. The doctors prescribed nausea-inducing agents for them, but told them the medication would help them to relieve their symptoms. The result was shocking: the subjects felt relieved after taking their prescription because their brains were able to manifest what they wanted their future outcomes to be.

THOUGHT: CAUSATION OF REALITY

When Lao Tzu said, "The journey of a thousand miles begins with a single step," he was only half right. Every action first starts with a thought and the rest is manifestation. As Emerson said, "The ancestor of every action is a thought."

Our world or circumstances are products and manifestations of our own thoughts. Our thoughts are the causes; our reality is the effects. We cannot change our circumstances without first changing our thinking. Here is a shocking example – On the anniversary of 911, the winning numbers from New York State Lottery are 911! An eerie coincidence? Certainly not. Thought is a powerful force that creates power and energy to bring about our mental pictures into manifestation.

There are conscious thoughts and subconscious thoughts. When we think in our mind, we are thinking consciously; while thinking in our heart, it is the subconscious that is in operation. When we think the same thoughts day-after-day, then these thoughts are sunk deep into our heart or subconscious mind. A repeated thinking pattern becomes a mental condition. In other words, we become what we think about. This means we must also cast out all doubt, shame, and other negative feelings, as they have the dangerous opportunity of pinning us down and keeping us from achieving our goals.

You have the power to press the reset button. All your opportunities can be manifested in your own terms as long as you have faith. Think from the wish fulfilled, and you are capable of achieving anything.

CONCLUSION

Knowledge is not power unless you apply it, just as faith without work is dead. It is often the hardest moments in our lives that teach us the most valuable lessons.

To transform your life during a time of crisis, you should practice the S.W.I.F.T. Transformation formula that is sure to work magic:

- Think *from* (not *of*) the wish fulfilled
- Imagine the end result (see it, hear it, and feel it)
- Fake it, make it, and become it
- Believe it is possible
- Declare your wish has come true

In conclusion, think of the wise old donkey from the parable who was determined to survive being buried in a pit. How does a wise creature shake off the dirt and step out of the pit?

…by pressing the reset button!

About George

George Lee, Esq. has a great passion to help people resolve legal, emotional, and life issues. As a successful attorney, he has been in and out of courtrooms fighting for justice for about two decades. As an accredited family law mediator, he motivates families to resolve their separation and divorce issues through amicable compromise.

Outside his legal career, George is also a Transformational coach. For many years, he has been passionate about inspiring clients to discover greatness from within, and to fulfil their life purpose and dreams.

In addition to a Juris Doctor degree from the University of Victoria in Canada, George earned a master's degree in English Literature. However, his learning journey never stopped there. He has continued to pursue studies in Life Coaching, Hypnotism, NLP, psychology, and spirituality. For many years, George learned from top leaders in the personal development field, including Richard Bandler, Tony Robbins, Brian Tracy, and Jack Canfield.

In recent years, George has created and practiced a system he coined as S.W.I.F.T. Transformation™ Coaching that involves the integration of five modalities, including **S**ense, **W**ord, **I**magination, **F**aith, and **T**hought. He coaches clients to practice the five transformational steps to effect changes in their subconscious mind.

George is in the process of finalizing his manuscript of his new book, tentatively entitled, *Be Transformed: Unveil Divine Secrets and Reclaim Your Super Powers*. His next task is to ensure his new book is published soon.

George speaks fluent Chinese, and, as such, his clientele spreads into Asia as well. He lives in Vancouver, Canada with his wife and children.

You can connect with George at:

- www.georgelee.ca
- www.gleelaw.com

CHAPTER 11

LOVE-LIFE'S ONLY VALUABLE EMOTION

BY SEEMA CHOUDHRI

All you need in life is love because love conquers all. Love is unconditional and selfless.

> *The wise are wise only because they love.*
> ~ Paulo Coelho

Love is the shining goal of every human soul. You will attract success, happiness and fulfillment in life once you cultivate this one simple form of emotion, LOVE. This is an emotion that encompasses interpersonal, cultural, social, physiological, political, professional and philosophical states of all human beings.

What is love at first sight? How does it happen? When did it begin?

The following extract illustrates this beautifully:

> The SERPENT: The voice in the garden is your own voice.
> ADAM: It is, and it is not. It is something greater than me. I am only a part of it.

THE ONE BIG THING

> EVE: No voice is needed to make me feel that.
> ADAM: (Throwing his arm around her in anguish) Oh no: that is plain without any voice. There is something, that holds us together something that has no word.
> THE SERPENT: . . . LOVE, LOVE, LOVE.

If you are looking for a happier and more direction-oriented life, the pages ahead will not only lead you there, but will also ensure you remain there your entire life. However, you must safeguard yourself from any sort of processing of this basic ingredient of ultimate success and victory.

All your life, you just need one word written on the flag of your success and achievements, LOVE. If you sit in peace and define success for yourself, love will inadvertently come to the fore. You will feel love in the deepest core of your heart and happiness will abound.

> *Seize the moments of happiness,*
> *Love and be Loved!*
> *That is the only reality in the world,*
> *All else is folly.*
> *~ Leo Tolstoy.*

Let this raw and nascent Love start with loving yourself.

> *To love oneself is the beginning of a lifelong romance!*
> *~ Oscar Wide*

THE MAGIC OF SELF-LOVE

LOVE-LIFE'S ONLY VALUABLE EMOTION

Learn to love yourself and all else will fall in place.

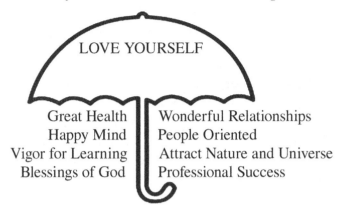

The major key to a better future is you.
~ Jim Rohn

Self-love is a pre-requisite for a good life. Since childhood we are conditioned to love others and keep justifying ourselves to others. It is only after we attain a certain level of maturity and experience, that we reflect upon loving our own selves. It is now that we are able to comprehend that the only validation and affirmation we need is from ourselves. In fact, this idea of loving ourselves first, brings in a sense of selfishness accompanied with guilt. On the contrary, however, a more holistic glance will divulge that this has more to do with self-fulness. Your cup is full, what flows out is for others. The essential idea however remains that your cup must be full.

INGREDIENTS OF SELF-LOVE

Six essential ingredients of Self-Love are:
1. <u>Self-knowing</u>: You commit to become your own best friend, get to know yourself through honest communication and sharing with your own self. You spend quiet time getting to know yourself through self-reflection and introspection. It is of worth to write down your thoughts and focus really on

yourself: What is it that you really like or don't like? What drags you and motivates you and what are your goals and dreams? What ideas would you share with your future self?

Seek answers to questions such as "Who is the real me?" Build an honest relationship with your own self. Be your best friend at all times and in doing so, try following a few steps, such as planning solo activities and spending time doing things alone, e.g., reading, yoga, music, hobbies, meditating, exercising. These will let you appreciate and enjoy your own company. Accepting and forgiving yourself is as important as comforting and encouraging yourself, especially in difficult times.

2. Self-attachment: You feel connected to yourself both physically as well as mentally. You desire and hope to form positive connections with everyone around you, but the fact remains that it is essential first to connect with your own self, before you seek outward connections.

3. Self-affection: You feel complete, happy and in total harmony with yourself. You invariably love being in your own company.

4. Unconditional and Positive Self-Regard: You stop the wish game: I wish I was this... If only I was that... How I wish I was taller, thinner, fairer, younger and so much more. Accept and encourage yourself, no matter what your status, no matter how many failures or successes.

5. Self-worth: You realise your true value: one to your ownself and your value in others' lives. The feeling that you are a gift of God on earth dominates your mindset.

6. Self-caring: This is both a component and an outcome of self love. The more you love yourself, the more you care for your physical as well as your mental wellbeing. Self-care is more

to do with your attitude – one which says, I am responsible for myself. Self-care helps prevent burnout, reduces stress and helps you focus on what is really important for you.

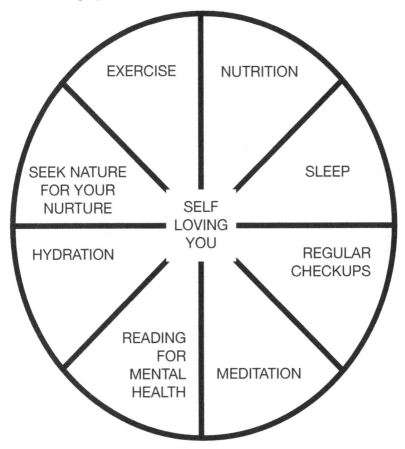

Self-loving people follow a daily healthcare regime.

To love oneself is the beginning of life-long romance.
~ Oscar Wilde

Remember, you are the protagonist of your greatest love story.

SELF-LOVE----> Be your own BFF (Best Friend Forever)

THE ONE BIG THING

As a self-loving person you protect yourself while entering new relationships, just like a best friend would do. In times of bad relationships, you standup for your own rights. You choose to listen to your best friend's advice and your best friend is right inside you.

Have you been in a situation or a relationship where you know there was something wrong, yet you stayed in it? Why did you do it? Just frequently use KWINK [Knowing What I Now Know] analysis, would I do it again? You will be amazed to see its effectiveness. Watch out for your response to the Kwink analysis, if it is a 'No', leave the situation as if you were to dash out of a building that has caught fire.

You will feel tremendous strength and courage in times of challenges or difficulties, which will help you recognize your mistakes and act upon them wisely. You will refuse to compromise your core values and beliefs and simply uphold your self-respect and self-worth.

SELF-LOVE------> Best Manifestations
  (a). **Love for learning**
    Love for learning has been propagated since time immemorial all over the world through the mythological deities associated with knowledge, wisdom or intelligence. For instance, Neith (Ancient Egyptian), Laozi (Chinese), Anahit (Armenian), Metis and Athena (Greek), Sarasvati (Hindu), and Benzaiten (Japanese) are all embodiments of knowledge, wisdom, music, art, nature, philosophy, creativity and learning.

Learning gives creativity,
Creativity leads to thinking,
Thinking provides knowledge,
Knowledge makes you GREAT.
~ A.P.J. Abdul Kalam

LOVE-LIFE'S ONLY VALUABLE EMOTION

Love for learning fills you with positive thinking, enlightenment and intellectuality. If you recall your childhood as a time spent studying several subjects for long hours, it is likely that you fell in the trap of the game of scoring higher and higher marks. You must not overlook distinguishing between studying and learning. Books, reading and learning scare many, including adults. They fail to realise that learning is the most powerful tool for promoting growth.

If you are not willing to learn,
No one can help you.
If you are determined to learn,
No one can stop you.
~ Zig Ziglar

Good habits are difficult to form, but easy to live with. Once you realise that the key to success lies in the love for learning and in the unending quest for knowledge, you automatically drift from the world of ignorance towards the world of wisdom. Books can be your favourite pastime, your best friends, philosophers and guides. Let the little spark of learning kindle in you, and you will soon find a never-extinguishing fire for learning inside you.

One small dose of motivational learning before you start your day will keep you and your entire day in great shape. You will be focused, clear and goal-oriented.

When we are kids we ask questions like
why is the sky blue, why is the bird flying so high.
For some reason as we grow older, that curiosity goes away.
If we are happy with what we know,
then we are actually going to atrophy.
So please remain a lifelong student...
don't lose that curiosity.
~ Indira Nooyi – Ex CEO Pepsi Co

Five must-read Books
-- *Man's Search for Meaning* ~ Victor E. Frankl
-- *The Power of Now* ~ Eckhart Tolle
-- *Ask and It Is Given* ~ Esther and Jerry Hicks
-- *The Power of Intention* ~ Dr Wayne W Dyer
-- *Don't Sweat the Small Stuff* ~ Richard Carlson

I have delved deep into philosophy and religion. Years of study and research have reinforced my belief in the CREATOR, our GOD.

You have been sent to this earth with a special purpose. It is because of this that you are unique and different from all others. You are endowed with remarkable qualities. When God designed your software, He made LOVE as the centre point from which all else emanated.

Belief, trust, faith and one-to-one relationship with the Almighty blossoms when LOVE is your mainstay. You do not question His ways. You have courage and strength to believe that whatever He is giving you is only to make you better and wiser.

This never-ending trust in the Almighty acts as a shield to protect you from the daily burnouts, keep you free from stress and anxiety, and help you foster an attitude of gratitude for all that you have.

  (b). **Love for work**

      Peace, happiness and joy are of paramount importance for a successful and fulfilled life. Choose to work only for your love and passion. Find all the ways and mechanisms to let your passions find you a living. Don't land up in a job, land up doing what you enjoy doing.

      Now your day is well planned in writing, and you are eager to learn more and add more not only in your organization, but also in your own professional expertise. You read books related to your career and learn and train yourself to be more effective. Since you are doing what you love, you feel charged-up and energetic. You are happy when you return home. You are able to boost the morale of your family members as you had a fulfilling and a satisfying day.

(c). **Love for family**
You will enjoy your home life and establish meaningful and wonderful relationships. People are essentially relationship-seeking organisms. They look for stability, smoothness, calmness and happiness in their close relationships. A heart full of love is positive, and optimistic wholehearted love, affection and dedication attract similar emotions from others around. Even on occasions when there is family distress, unhappiness and instability, your love, dedication and affection would facilitate happy, vibrant and positive thoughts amongst them.

A being who is contented and satisfied with him/herself is motivated, forward-looking, kind, sincere and committed. You are able to keep your entire home in great energy when 'your own cup is full'.

The bond that links your true family is not one of blood, but of love, respect and joy.
~ Richard Bach

I was not yet in love, yet I loved to love...
I sought what I might love, in love with loving.
~ St. Augustine of Hippo

CONCLUSION

A loving heart is people oriented, bountiful, generous and full of empathy for every living soul around. You do not merely live by default. Today, people are surrounded with so many machines that sensitivity and human touch, which are so vital to life, are altogether missing. Let us strive towards the day when wealth is equitably distributed and all demarcations of rich and poor are eliminated. A little effort on the part of each one of us will certainly make a world of difference.

Many will be fed, sheltered and helped to live more respectful lives and contribute to the upliftment of mankind.

A heart full of love radiates itself on the outward appearance of a person. You look serene, calm and confident.

LOVE: Life's Only Valuable Emotion

You have no time and energies to waste criticizing yourself or others. Instead of pulling yourself or others down, transform yourself into a power house of energy and a rich resource that people can look-up to.

> In my life, I've lived, I've learned, I've lost,
> I've missed, I've hurt, I've trusted,
> I've made mistakes, but most of all...
> I've loved.

You will always find what you are looking for, so if you look for fear you will attract insecurity. On the other hand, if you look for LOVE inside yourself, you will perceive, find, create and foster it.

Once your inner world (over which you have 100% control) is full of love, you will attract energies that are congruent to it in the outer world. You will attract success, good relationships, fame, comforts, happiness and fortune. Your inner as well as outer peace, harmony and ecstasy is not only ensured but guaranteed.

About Seema

Writer, counsellor, and an entrepreneur, Seema Choudhri is a scholar in Psychology, Counselling and Therapy from Oxford University, London. A certified career counselor alumnus of Loreto Convent, Lucknow, India, she has also qualified for UGC - JRF. In the early years of her career, she was designated as a Lecturer at Amity University, a well-acclaimed institution in the early 2000s.

With an expertise in creating original works, proposing counselling topics, gathering information on the topic, and selecting and organizing the material, she has been successful in propounding new ideas to bring about significant changes in the education industry for two decades.

With a keen interest in personal empowerment, she embarked upon two educational ventures with the underlying aim of propagating the need for guidance for any child to pursue her dreams. The first was **C.A.R.E.** (Centre for Advance Research in Education) – her first stint which promotes skill-development courses. The second is **I.R.E.C.** (International Research & Education Council) which aims at behavioral, emotional and career counselling at large. With proficiency in writing and editing, adhering to set standards regarding order, clarity, conciseness, style and terminology in accordance with any defined framework, she is known for devising various learning and training courses.

Seema has been scouting for material on various subjects and identification of Scholars & Experts who could enrich the proposed project, organizing initiatives for gathering inputs on specialized subjects. Acknowledged for framing the training objectives based on training needs after assessment of the gap between skills already available and desired, she has been mentoring students towards their coveted goals in the form of quantifiable units.

Seema Choudhri is an insightful Speaker and Success Expert trained at Success Mastery Academy, California. Her mission is to empower the next generation to tread on the path they excel in, and choose the right career ahead. She has always been a keen planner and implementer with a track record for developing operational policies/norms, systems and controls, and schemes and educational standards for professionals/students.

Quickly building rapport with audiences through her unique combination of light-hearted life experiences and enthusiasm, she is deft at delivering high-end technical lectures at various forums. Seema Choudhri has been a keynote speaker at numerous conferences. Through her teaching and professional guidance, she has helped thousands of individuals to choose the right path with ease.

She possesses dexterity in deploying the right research tools in the field, collecting prime information with industry experts and report presentations. She has a proven track record of mapping the latest trends of learning content design and shaping them up through innovative ideas. She is a perfectionist with an eye for details and an in-depth understanding of content development standards and instructional techniques.

Her book talks about how an instance in her life led to a series of changes – material and immaterial – which shaped her into the personality she is. It throws light on the various shades of life and how we can use the minutest nuances of our lives to bring out the best in us.

She would love to hear from you at:

- joywithcare@gmail.com
- counselling.irec@gmail.com
- www.irec4u.com

CHAPTER 12

PAINFREE ... WOW!™ THE SHORTCUT TO INSTANT PAIN ELIMINATION

BY DR. THAY JOE TAN

First of all ... Congratulations!
... for buying this book,
... for reading this chapter,
... for taking your time, as reading the following pages will change YOUR life and the lives of those you care about.

It will be the most rewarding time you will have ever spent reading on the topic of pain ... or better, pain elimination ... or even better ... INSTANT pain elimination.

How do I know that? Because this is the very first of many books to come where I will reveal the best kept (unknown) secret about instant pain elimination. It's so secret that even insiders don't know.

ESPECIALLY FOR YOU

Although I dedicate this book to my beloved Mom, who is in her eighties now, this book is especially for YOU.

THE ONE BIG THING

Nothing in life happens by accident, but everything happens for a special reason, at the right time, at the right place and with the right people. If you read these pages, something must have attracted you to do so. Most likely, you are somebody who suffers from pain or who has family or friends suffering from pain.

Alternatively, maybe you are a doctor or professional who serves patients in one way or another, perhaps as a medical or naturopathic doctor, doctor of alternative, oriental, Chinese or other medicine, chiropractor or osteopath, acupuncturist, dentist, homeopath, nurse, doula, massage therapist or "healer" of any kind.

Whether you are a patient or a doctor, after reading these pages, you will know that there is a simple way to eliminate pain instantly – a shortcut. And once you know that, you might want to blow this knowledge out into the world for the benefit of all people in pain (80 million in the USA alone, hundreds of millions worldwide), so that they can be released from their suffering, enjoy an active life again and claim their birthright to be painfree.

Yes, being painfree is a birthright!

WHAT DOES *INSTANT PAIN ELIMINATION* MEAN?

Well, *pain elimination* means bringing any kind of pain from a scale between one and ten down to zero. That is pain *elimination* in contrast to pain *reduction*. 100% pain *reduction* would equal pain *elimination*. So, it really means pain *release*, not merely pain *relief.*

Instant means immediately or within a few seconds. Thirty seconds or a minute would already be long ... but still pretty good for somebody who has been suffering from pain for months, years and decades, don't you think so?

IS THIS MAGIC?

Let me give you a typical example. A patient enters my practice with a severe migraine headache. I insert a tiny acupuncture needle in her foot, and then ask the patient, "How does it feel?" The patient responds, "What do you mean?" And I say, "Well, you said you had a headache. How is your headache?" The patient replies, "Why? Have you done anything yet?" I say, "Yes, I put a needle into your foot." The patient responds, "Oh yes, really? But ... it cannot work that fast, can it?" I reply, "Absolutely it can. So how is your headache?" The patient says, "Well, actually it's gone ... Wow! ... this is a miracle! Are you a wizard?" I say, "No, I'm not a wizard." The patient responds, "But this is like magic!" And then I explain, "Yes, indeed it's like magic. But magic becomes logic, if you know the HOW and the WHY. So, if you watch a magician pull a rabbit out of a hat, it's like magic. But if the magician revealed to you the secret of how he did it, you would say you can do it too, right?"

Theoretically, what I described above could happen to any patient in pain and could happen to any doctor treating a patient in pain. Of course, the doctor needs to know how to do it. You will read more about this later, and also in forthcoming books of the *Painfree ... Wow!*™ series.

HOW ALL BEGAN

Coming from a family of doctors (not that my parents were doctors, but many of my cousins, aunts, and uncles were), my mother wanted me to become a doctor. Finally, after finishing high school, I didn't know anything better to do, and seeing that my relatives who were doctors were all doing quite well, I thought, why not?

So, I went to Medical University and graduated in 1991. During the following years, I gained valuable experience in treating acute and chronic disorders including pain – whether as a Junior

Doctor in the UK, as a doctor serving in the German Federal Armed Forces or being deeply involved in emergency medical work during on-call assignments for general practitioners or medical specialists of any kind.

Different to most doctors who choose to get trained in any of the medical specialties, I decided to study dentistry instead. And here is where I had my key moment regarding acupuncture that should change my life, the life of my patients, and ultimately the world.

THE TURNING POINT

One day during my dentistry studies, I observed a dentist performing acupuncture on a patient who was hyper-salivating and retching. Shortly after inserting the needles, the excessive salivation ceased and the patient calmed down, so the dentist could continue with the initial dental procedure.

Seeing this, I was so amazed that I immediately decided to learn acupuncture.

Having been trained in Western medicine and dentistry, learning Chinese medicine and acupuncture was like entering a new world—a beautiful world which explained how the human body works from a different perspective. Furthermore, it also explained the correlation between the human body and nature in a very clear and logical way. I was fascinated!

After two years, I received my first acupuncture diploma, and after another five years, my second.

THE DISCOVERY

Fast forward over the past 20+ years, I had the privilege to acquire deep knowledge and precious wisdom of Chinese philosophy and medicine from countless professors and teachers from all over the world. Combining and refining the best of their best and most effective methods and techniques, I discovered one day that needling one single acupuncture point can eliminate pain instantly; of course, it needs to be the right one.

So the knowledge of only twelve (out of several hundreds of) acupuncture points is sufficient to control almost the entire body. How cool is that! This was really like discovering the Holy Grail of pain medicine.

Because this treatment method is so powerful and fast acting, I named it *Turbo*Acupuncture™, and I named the twelve points *Turbo*Acupuncture™ points. I saw the need to name it differently, as it really outperforms normal acupuncture in speed, simplicity, and impact.

This was by far the biggest discovery in my entire professional life, MY ONE BIG THING. And if I had to start all over again, and I was allowed to learn only one thing, I would definitely choose *Turbo*Acupuncture™, as with the minimal investment of one weekend, I can have maximum impact on patients' well-being. I can become the master of the game ... the game called *Instant Pain Elimination*. And this unique skill of instant pain elimination would be my single most valuable asset.

As I had discovered this unique system to eliminate pain instantly with just ONE needle, I wanted to find a way to make *Turbo*Acupuncture™ available to all pain patients. So, I condensed my compound knowledge and expertise in Chinese medicine and acupuncture that I had acquired over more than two decades, distilled the essence of it and developed a system to teach any doctor the art of instant pain elimination in just ONE weekend.

Yes, you read correctly. Every doctor without prior knowledge of acupuncture can learn *Turbo*Acupuncture™ in just ONE weekend.

PAIN ELIMINATION IS LIKE A GAME

Pain elimination is like a game, even more so is INSTANT pain elimination. If you want to win the game, first of all, you need to understand the game.

> *You Need To Know The Rules Of The Game ...*
> *And Then Play It Better Than Anybody Else.*
> ~ Albert Einstein

With the understanding of pain according to mainstream Western medicine, it goes as far as it gets ... leaving hundreds of millions of people behind suffering from pain—80 million pain patients in the USA alone.

But ... according to classical Chinese medical literature, the answer to the question, "Where does pain come from and how can it be treated?" was already given a few thousand years ago.

THE BLOCKED WATER HOSE

Chinese medicine says that pain occurs when the flow of the vital energy Qi is blocked, or the flow of blood is blocked, or both Qi and blood are blocked.

Basically, it's like a blocked water hose. Imagine you have a flexible water hose that you can bend and stretch. If water is flowing through it, everything is fine. However, if the water hose gets blocked and the water cannot flow anymore, that equals pain.

So, what can you do to unblock the water hose so that the water can flow freely again? Well, yes, you could stretch, bend, or twist the water hose. Maybe that is good enough to remove the blockage and let the water flow freely again. You could also tap on it or apply some vibration to it. Maybe that does the job.

The aforementioned is comparable to stretching, massaging,

tapping, or vibrating the painful part of the body. Maybe it helps release or at least relieve the pain. If not, what could you do next? Yes, exactly. You could flush out the water hose. That's what *Turbo*Acupuncture™ does.

And that's why it's possible that pain can be eliminated instantly, in the same way that a blocked water hose can be unblocked.

THE REVOLUTION IN PAIN MEDICINE

Here's why *Turbo*Acupuncture™ is so revolutionary and why it will cause a paradigm shift in pain medicine, becoming the NEW Gold Standard for Pain Elimination:

1. One tiny needle inserted hardly one millimeter in the correct place makes all the difference between a person in pain and the same person without pain.
2. It can be learned by any doctor in ONE weekend.
3. It saves big money spent on painkillers and other medicine, sick leave, diagnostic imaging, operations, rehabilitation.
4. It has practically no contraindications.
5. It has practically no side effects.
6. The cost of material is negligible.
7. It can be performed anywhere (e.g. on a plane), even without undressing the patient.
8. It works reliably for almost any kind of pain, no matter if it is acute, chronic or complex – such as (but not limited to):

    - Headache incl. migraine and trigeminal neuralgia
    - Neck pain
    - Back pain
    - Sciatica
    - Joint pain
    - Abdominal pain
    - Menstrual pain
    - Genital pain
    - Nerve pain
    - Muscle pain

- Bone pain
- CRPS (Chronic Regional Pain Syndrome)

Only in few cases it might not help (so much or so fast), such as:

- Severe prolapse of vertebral discs
- Severe deficiency of energy or blood
- Concomitant psychoemotional disorders

But even then, I would give it a chance, certainly before taking strong or long-term medication, or before considering any interventional type of pain therapy, including surgery.

THE DIFFERENCE: ONE NEEDLE ... ONE WEEKEND ...

So, the bottom line is:

- The difference between a person in pain and the same person without pain is *ONE needle*.

- The difference between a doctor who knows how to achieve this and a doctor who doesn't is *ONE weekend*.

Humanity is so close to pain no longer being a problem.

So only because people don't know this and doctors don't know, hundreds of millions of people need to suffer from pain (80 million in the USA alone) ... most of them totally unnecessary.

TOO GOOD TO BE TRUE?

Well, you can open your mind, believe it or not, and give it a try ... and this I forecast: You will experience your miracle, whether you are the pain patient finding a certified *Turbo*Acupuncture™ practitioner close by, or you are the doctor practicing *Turbo*Acupuncture™.

*What The Mind Can Conceive,
Man Can Achieve.*
~ Napoleon Hill

Alternatively, you can doubt it, distrust all the (video) testimonials about *Turbo*Acupuncture™ and nothing will change for you, which means you keep your pain if you're the patient, or you keep underdelivering if you are the doctor.

MY WISH FOR YOU

Experience the simplicity, beauty and true power of *Turbo*Acupuncture™.

Simplicity Is The Key To Brilliance.
~ Bruce Lee

If you suffer from pain, claim your birthright of being painfree. You're only ONE needle away!

If you are a doctor or acupuncturist, get your full therapeutic capacity and release your pain patients from their sufferings. You're only ONE weekend away!

Being Painfree Is A Birthright.

[Legal disclaimer: The aforementioned reflects the personal experience of the author. No guarantee of healing or feeling better is given.]

About Dr. Thay Joe Tan

Dr. Thay Joe Tan, MD, PhD, DMD is a multiple international award-winning Acupuncture Expert on Instant Pain Elimination. He is the Founder of *Turbo*Acupuncture™ for Instant Pain Elimination and the Founder and Director of one of Europe's largest physician-led practices for acupuncture based in Stuttgart, Germany, which has been awarded *Pain Elimination and Global Doctor Training Center of the Year 2019*.

Dr. Tan is the Creator of the T.A.N. (*Turbo*Acupuncture™ Navigation) system, which leads like a GPS from the location of pain step-by-step to THE one *Turbo*Acupuncture™ point, which will most likely eliminate the pain instantly.

Before starting his own private practice, he was a Senior Resident and the temporary Deputy of the Medical Director of the First German Hospital for Traditional Chinese Medicine, University Hospital at Beijing, University of Chinese Medicine in Kötzting, Germany.

Dr. Tan is the first person outside China who was ever granted the Inherited Master Fellowship of Qi Lu School of TCM for Complex Diseases, one of 64 acknowledged inherited schools of TCM in China.

His superpower in instant pain elimination, using only one acupuncture point, earned him multiple international awards such as *Acupuncture Specialist of the Year 2018, Instant Pain Elimination Expert of the Year 2019, Acupuncture Expert of the Year 2019* and *Acupuncturist of the Year 2019*. This skill elevates Dr. Thay Joe Tan to the forefront as THE Leading Authority for Instant Pain Elimination and predestines him to be the Key Opinion Leader in Pain Therapy.

Dr. Tan is also an author, international trainer, and speaker. His expertise has been valued at Beijing University of Chinese Medicine, United Nations Headquarters, a US Military Hospital and by audiences of over 1200 people. He is a Council Member of the Global Entrepreneurship Initiative® and the National Association of Experts, Writers and Speakers®.

Dr. Tan is also an exceptionally gifted, passionate, and enthusiastic teacher, who instructs doctors and other health professionals around the globe in

ONE weekend on how to eliminate pain instantly with just ONE needle. His *Turbo*Acupuncture™ Certification Masterclass has been awarded **Acupuncture Seminar of the Year 2019**. He is also the Founder and Director of The Global Painfree ... Wow!™ Doctors Initiative, which focuses on doctors to get rid of their pain.

Among his students are Medical and Naturopathic Doctors, as well as advanced acupuncturists with decades of experience. He even shared his knowledge with Chinese Doctors and Professors, who all experience their WOW moment when they suddenly discover the simplicity, beauty, and TRUE power of *Turbo*Acupuncture™.

Furthermore, he helps therapists to fast-start and grow their practice within 30 days or less. He supports hospitals worldwide implement *Turbo*Acupuncture™ as THE New Gold Standard for Instant Pain Elimination. He also supports and conducts mission trips. Dr. Tan welcomes cooperation with Medical Universities and Health Political Influencers.

As a native German of Chinese origin trained in conventional Western medicine and dentistry as well as in Chinese medicine, Dr. Tan understands how to integrate the intelligent power and elegance of Chinese medicine into the setting of mainstream Western medicine.

Dr. Tan is the Host and Chairman of the 1st World Summit on *Turbo*Acupuncture™ for Instant Pain Elimination – September 13-15, 2019 – in Stuttgart, Germany.

Website: www.painfreewow.com

[Legal disclaimer: The aforementioned reflects the personal experience of the author. No guarantee of healing or feeling better is given.]

NEED A KEYNOTE SPEAKER FOR YOUR EVENT?

We have thousands of Best-Selling Authors and Experts ready to share with your audience!

Contact Impact Speakers Group today, we'd love to help!
ImpactSpeakersGroup.com

iMPACT | Speakers Group